D1179299

Dictionary of
The Wild West

BROCKHAMPTON PRESS
LONDON

This edition published 1997 by Brockhampton Press, a member of the
Hodder Headline PLC Group

ISBN 1 86019 724 8

Printed and bound in India

Introduction

The Wild West is a source of fascination to many people. This fact is obvious from the sheer number of books and films that have been created around the theme. However, a great many of these works of fiction have done a disservice to the West in that they have romanticized it. For example, Roy Rogers and the other singing cowboys have little relevance to the hardship that was central to the life of the average cowboy.

The romance of the West has absorbed many writers. They have fallen in love with the idea of the wide, open spaces and the idea of Man against Nature, not to mention the fascination of the new start away from it all, and they have not always troubled to temper this romance with reality.

Many of the writers who lived through the pioneering days of the West were carried away with the imagined excitement and adventure without actually having experienced any of it. They simply based their stories on what they had heard and added a bit of poetic licence. The result is that fact and fiction have become intermingled in the story of the West. Some stories have some kind of basis in fact but they have become embellished and exaggerated out of all semblance of truth. Often it is difficult to extricate the facts from the fiction.

Thus we know that outlaws like Billy the Kid, Jesse James and Wesley Hardin existed and that their crimes were great, but often the number of people whom these outlaws are supposed to have killed have been grossly overestimated. Sometimes this is due to the fact that such people became legends in their own lifetime and they themselves added to the embellishment and exaggeration of the facts.

Certainly the West did in reality have a number of aspects that seemed to be the stuff of which legend and romance are made, especially from the point of view of a sophisticated readership sitting in the safety of its own sitting room—the wagon treks across country, the city dwellers facing the exciting challenge of starting their own farms or ranches under the Homestead scheme, the satisfaction of growing one's own crops and raising one's own livestock, the prospectors hurrying to join the gold-rushes in expectation of making a fortune.

But this was simply one side of the coin. On the other was the length and tedium of the journey, the dust, the flies, the disease, the extremes of temperature, the lack or sameness of the food and the lack of privacy of the wagon trek. In the course of the journey there was the very real danger of attacks from Indians and, unlike in the films, they were not always on the losing side.

When the Promised Land was reached, there was the nostalgia for home and family, the backbreaking work involved in building a house, fencing off the land and tilling the fields, the problems of raising livestock without any experience, the hostility of the large ranch owners who wanted the use of the ranges for themselves and resented the presence of homesteaders, and the stark realization that it was too far to go home.

The expectations of the prospectors likewise were usually far from being realized, their dreams of finding gold often meeting with nothing but difficult physical conditions, a lack of necessary equipment, danger from falling rocks and collapsing mines, or danger from Indians.

Of course there are many success stories in the history of the West, but hardship and failure were part of it too. It is important to remember that, although the opening up of the West spelt opportunity for some white settlers, it spelt the end of a way of life for the Native American Indians and the destruction of many animals, such as the beaver.

A

ABBEY, EDWARD

Edward Abbey (1927–1989) was an author who wrote a wide range of fiction and nonfiction on themes relating to the southwest. Several of his works deal with cowboys, particularly cowboys in their fight to preserve the traditional values and environment of the West against the threat of industrial modernity. His cowboy novels include *The Brave Cowboy* (1956) and *Fire on the Mountain* (1962) and a science-fiction work entitled *Good News*.

ABBOTT, EDWARD C.

Edward C. Abbott (1860–1939) was better known as Teddy Blue Abbott. He was both a cowboy and a writer. In 1871 he moved with his family from England to Nebraska where his father had bought a homestead where he planned to raise cattle. On accompanying his father on a trip to Texas to buy a herd of a cattle, a trip that involved driving the cattle across country all the way back to Nebraska, riding horseback and camping under the stars, the young Abbott decided that he was going to be a cowboy rather than be a farmer or rancher like his father. At eighteen he left home and did just that.

He was involved in some of the big cattle drives that had begun in the West after the Civil War, although these were coming to an end by the early 1890s. In these cattle drives, herds of long-horn cattle were driven from Texas to places such as Kansas, from which beef was then transported by train to the cities in the eastern parts of America, or to places such as Nebraska and Wyoming where huge cattle ranches were set up.

In his life as a cowboy on cattle trails, Abbot soon came to realize that the career of a cowboy was a hard one and not at all glamorous, as it is so often depicted in Hollywood movies. It was not a life of gambling, drinking, shooting and fighting Indians but a life of hard slog, dust, inclement weather conditions, lack of water, lack of sleep, low pay, bad food and the ever-present danger of stampeding cattle.

In 1883 Abbott decided to switch from the hard life of the cowboy to the life of a ranch-hand. Not only had he had enough of life on the cattle trail but its days were coming to an end. Railways were expanding and could transport cattle far more quickly than cowboys could, and the farmers who had been moving West to start homesteads were passing laws to stop cattle being driven through their land and destroying their crops.

Life as a ranch-hand was easier than life on the cattle trail but it was still far from being a life of ease. The ranches were remote from towns, the pay was still low and the annual cattle roundup when cows were branded and some cattle sent to market was extremely hard work.

Just as Abbott experienced the closing years of the long cattle trail, so he also experienced the end of the open ranges that were once so much a part of the American West. The open range consisted of extensive unfenced land owned by the government. Ranchers used the open range as a source of free grass for their cattle and turned their herds on to them all the year round, sending their ranch-hands out to check on them from time to time. The bitter winter of 1886, however, changed things fundamentally, for hundreds of thousands of cattle died as a result of the severe weather conditions. From then on cattle ranchers put up more fencing and, instead of leaving their cattle to roam free all year round, gathered them in during the winter to feed them.

At this point Abbot decided to become a homesteader, as his father had been, dying at the age of seventy-eight.

He was extremely concerned about the romantic view of cowboys and their lives, which was projected in films. For years he tried to interest people in his memories of life on the cattle trail and on the range but these were not in line with the gun-toting image of the cowboy which people were looking for and so he was unsuccessful.

Eventually he came across someone who was interested in his memoirs. She was a young writer from New York named Helena Huntington Smith. She helped him to put his memoirs together and the results of their joint efforts were published as *We Pointed Them North* (1939), which did much to explode the popular myth of the cowboy.

ABILENE

Abilene is a town in Kansas. Partly because of its position near the end of the rail line of the Kansas Pacific it was regarded by the cattlemen in the 1860s as a an ideal centre for them. Not only did it have a railroad, it had a river where cattle could drink and miles of grassy plains where they could graze and the end of a long cattle trail. It was far enough away from settled Kansas farming country, provided a good market for beef and had a nearby fort, Fort Riley, which could offer the cattlemen protection from the Indians. Joseph McCoy did much to turn Abilene into a cow town. This was not by any means a good thing for the people of Abilene because the early cowboys there were lawless and the town had to employ a marshal to try to keep them in check. The second marshal of Abilene was the well-known 'Wild Bill' Hickok. *See* ELLSWORTH; HICKOK, WILD BILL; and WICHITA.

ACHEY, MARY ELIZABETH

Among the artists associated with the West are several women. There were more than a thousand women artists and art teachers in the West by 1890. Of the women artists, a noted example is Mary Elizabeth Achey. The earliest of her drawings were executed when she was accompanying her husband who was in the army. Not surprisingly, some of her early sketches were of frontier posts.

Tragedy struck when her only daughter died of a fever. Mary Achey was mad with grief and blamed her husband for the death of their daughter. She left him and spent the rest of her life until her death at the age of fifty-three travelling around the West. All this time she was painting and her output was considerable. Indeed, she is considered to have been the most prolific woman artist in the West in the period from 1860 until 1885 when she died.

ADAMS, ANDY
Andy Adams (1859–1935) was a cowboy and a writer. Many fiction writers have tended to write about what became the Hollywood stereotype of the hard-drinking, gun-toting cowboy but Adams, knowing about the real-life's cowboy's circumstances from personal experience, was much more realistic. He wrote *The Log of a Cowboy* (1903), which, in the form of a novel, recounted some of his experiences.

It uses some poetic licence but is much more true-to-life than most novels in the cowboy genre, describing among other things the horror of the cattle trail.

ADAMS, CLIFTON
Clifton Adams (1919–) is a novelist who specializes in writing novels with a Western theme. He has written under various names.

ADAMS, RAMON FREDERICK
Ramon Adams (1889–1976) was originally a concert violinist and then, after a broken arm brought his musical career to a pre-

mature end, the owner of a sweet-making business. However his hobby was a very important part of his life, and this centred on the American West, particularly outlaws.

He wrote *The Old-Time Cowhand* (1961) and *Come an' Get It: The Story of the Old Cowboy Cook*, but is best remembered as a bibliographer of publications relating to cowboys. In addition he is remembered as a lexicographer who specialized in words associated with the West. He is the author of *Cowboy Lingo* (1936) and *Western Words* (1944; expanded edition 1968).

Ramon Adams was also known as a thorn in the flesh to writers about the American West who were not careful enough about their research and who got their facts wrong. He was extremely critical of them and they resented his criticism,.

ADAIR, CORDELIA *see* ADAIR, JOHN.

ADAIR, JOHN

John Adair was an Irish financier who gave backing to Charles Goodnight when he set up a ranch in the Palo Duro Canyon. This became known as JA Ranch, JA being John Adair's initials, and was a million and a quarter acres in extent. It was extremely profitable and Goodnight tried his hand at crossbreeding cattle and introduced white-faced Herefords to the West, a venture that proved very successful.

Adair was content to leave the running of the ranch to Goodnight, preferring to remain in eastern America. On Adair's death, however, his wife Cordelia took to going west to check on her investment, always being accompanied by a retinue of maids and butlers and a huge amount of personal baggage and luxury goods from the east. In 1890 Goodnight withdrew from the JA Ranch to invest in a new ranch for himself, Cordelia Adair having proved to be a competent rancher. *See* GOODNIGHT, CHARLES.

ADOBE WALLS

Adobe Walls was the scene of a battle in the Texas Panhandle between buffalo hunters and Indians of the southern plains in 1874. In the battle more than five hundred Indians attacked a trading post where about thirty-five buffalo hunters were staying. The Indians, led by Quanah of the Comanches, had thought to mount a surprise attack, but Billy Dixon, a famous Texas scout, was awakened by a noise and spotted the assembled Indians along the edge of the creek.

He had scarcely time to wake the others before the Indians swooped down. Despite their superior numbers, and despite the surprise element in their attack, the Indians were defeated. The action lasted five days and yet Quanah and his men could not get into the doors of the stockade. The main reason for the defeat was the long-range game weapons held by the buffalo hunters, against which the weapons of the Indians could not compete. *See* PARKER, QUANAH.

AFRICAN AMERICANS *see* EXODUSTERS.

ALAMO

The Alamo was the name of an ancient mission station in San Antonio which became very famous in American history thanks to the role that it played in the Mexican War. The leader of the Mexicans, Santa Anna, laid siege to the Alamo in February 1836. The odds against the Texans who were defending the Alamo were immense. They numbered fewer than two hundred while Santa Anna's army numbered around six thousand.

The Texan garrison at the Alamo asked in vain for reinforcements before the attack began, but they were told to abandon the station. They decided to stay and make a stand against the Mexicans, despite the overwhelming odds, and managed to hold out for about ten days. Santa Anna became aware of just how small the defending force was and mounted a particularly strong offensive which the Texans could not repel.

All but the noncombatants in the mission station were killed and burned on two funeral pyres.

The Texans lost the siege of the Alamo but it is remembered for the great courage and determination shown by those who took part in it. These included Jim Bowie, brother of Rezin Bowie, who had invented the Bowie knife, William Barrett Travis and Davy Crockett. The noncombatants at the siege had their lives spared by the Mexicans, and it was they who told of the courage of the defenders, a courage that was to become legendary.

The siege was to become a proud part of American history. It was also to make the Texans even more determined to win against the Mexicans.

ALLISON, CLAY

Clay Allison (1840–87) fought on the Confederate side in the American Civil War and was discharged from the Tennessee Light Infantry after receiving a blow to his head that rendered him epileptic and is thought to have made him mentally deranged. He became a rancher and a cowboy and became notorious for his violent gunfighting escapades, especially when he was suffering from the effects of alcohol.

Various legends about him exist. According to one of these, he once stripped naked and rode through a Texan town wearing nothing but his holster and guns. Another story has him leading a lynch mob against a man named Kennedy who was a mass murderer who was guilty of infanticide, the victim perhaps having been his own daughter. Allison is said to have cut off Kennedy's head and ridden with it to a nearby saloon.

In another story about him we find Allison in a fast-draw gun contest with a fellow gunman named Mace Bowman. Allison is said to have suggested that he and Bowman strip off to their underwear and shoot at each other's feet to see who danced more energetically under this form of gunfire. Apparently neither seem to have been hurt in this contest.

Another Allison story involves Wyatt Earp. Allison is said to have ridden into Dodge City in Kansas with a view to wreaking havoc. Wyatt Earp was marshal there and succeeded in getting his gun pressed against Allison's ribs before he could use his drawn gun. Allison decided it was politic to leave town.

According to another legend, Allison was due to settle a dispute in rather a bizarre way. He and the other man involved in the dispute had arranged to fight a duel absolutely naked in a grave, the fight being conducted with Bowie knives and the winner having the privilege of engraving the tombstone. Before this extraordinary duel could take place, however, Allison was to die rather a bizarre death.

He was apparently driving to his ranch from Pecos in Texas where he had gone for supplies. When a sack of grain fell off the wagon he leaned over to try and retrieve the sack and toppled over off the wagon. A wagon wheel went over his neck and brought to an end the life of this notorious character.

AMERICAN FUR COMPANY
The American Fur Company was formed by John Jacob Astor in 1803. *See* ASTOR, JOHN JACOB.

ANDERSON, 'BLOODY BILL'
Bill Anderson, known as 'Bloody Bill' Anderson, was a gunman who took part in the guerrilla warfare that existed on the borders of Kansas and Missouri in the 1850s and 1860s. He was part of the band of men, led by William Quantrill, who attacked and destroyed the town of Lawrence, Kansas, in 1863. Later he became leader of his own band of men, two of his gang members being Frank James and Jesse James.

ANGUS, SHERIFF 'RED'

'Red' Angus was sheriff of Buffalo at the time of the Johnson County War. When rumours, and then confirmation, of the planned invasion of Johnson County reached him in Buffalo and having failed to get any offers of help from the state militia or from the regular army troops stationed at nearby Fort McKinney, Angus organized a makeshift army of homesteaders to augment his small regular posse.

At that time the invaders, known as the Regulators, under the leadership of Major Wolcott, were preparing to march towards Buffalo. They had spent the night about fourteen miles from the town at the TA Ranch and when scouts warned them of the advance of Sheriff Angus and his strange army they decided not to press forward but to remain at the TA Ranch and fortify as well as they could by building a barricade and digging trenches.

Their makeshift fort proved effective and the battle had lasted for two days when Arapaho Brown, an Indian fighter who had joined Red Angus, suggested smoking the inhabitants of the ranch out by surrounding a bundle of dynamite with bales of hay mounted on a wagon. Just as they were about to direct this device towards the ranch, three troops of the Sixth Cavalry arrived and saved the Regulators, Wolcott having succeeded in getting one of his scouts across the homesteaders' lines to go to Fort McKinney.

The commander of the cavalry troops refused to turn the Regulators over to Red Angus or any of the Johnson County authorities, much to the annoyance of their sheriff. They were taken to Fort DA Russell and were held for some time awaiting trial, the costs for their food and guards being charged to Johnson County. When Johnson County came to the end of its resources, the Regulators were taken back to Cheyenne where their imprisonment was just a sham. In January 1893 the case against them was dismissed. *See* Johnson County War.

APACHES

The Apaches were the North American Indians who were native to Arizona and New Mexico. They were a warlike people who resented the intrusion of the white man into their terrain and were not slow to demonstrate this. Noted for their stealth, cunning and for the suddenness of their attacks, they provided a great deal of opposition to those who would take over their land. The Apaches were a strong, brawny people who prided themselves on their powers of endurance, and leadership of the Apache tribes was dependent on individual initiative.

Mangas Colorados

Problems between the white men and the Apaches began in the late 1850s when Mangas Colorados, a chief of the Chiricahua tribe, visited the miners at Pinos Altos in the southwest of New Mexico. Although it was a friendly visit, the miners attacked him by tying him to a tree and bull-whipping him. He was naturally extremely angry and to get revenge sought the help of Cochise, who was not only his son-in-law but one of the great Chiricahua warrior chiefs. Thus began a war.

Cochise

In fact Cochise soon had his own grudge against the white men because early in 1861 he was accused of kidnapping a white boy named Ward. The accusation was false as the boy had been stolen by a member of the Pinal Apaches, but George Bascom of the Seventh Cavalry refused to believe in Cochise's innocence. He arranged for Cochise and his family to be taken hostage, but Cochise slashed the tent in which he was being held and escaped. He them took several white people hostage with a view to exchanging them for his relatives and friends who were being held by Bascom. Bascom refused, Cochise killed his white hostages and Bascom hanged three of his India hostages.

Cochise went to war with the white men with a vengeance.

He and his braves attacked ranches and mines and ambushed wagon trains. The Chiricahua Apaches were able to take advantage of the civil conflict that was by then raging in America, since many of the troops who would normally have inhabited the region were away fighting.

Apache Pass
At the conflict centred on Apache Pass (1862), Mangas Colorados was shot in the chest as he retreated. His injury made him tired of fighting a short time later and he decided to go alone to Pinos Altos and take the Americans up on their overtures of peace. His treatment by the guards there, acting under the instructions of General Joseph West, incensed Cochise even further and he continued with his campaign against the white men, torturing them as he went. This torture took the form of cutting small pieces of the body away until the victim bled to death as well as dragging people behind horses at the end of lariats until they died.

General Granger was sent to try to make peace with the Apaches, and many of them took up his offer of a life in a reservation in the mountains and valleys of Tularosa. Cochise and his warriors refused and went back to Arizona.

Camp Grant
Other Apaches, however, namely the Arivaipa Apaches, went to Camp Grant to ask the commander to give them a refuge where they could live in peace. This they were granted, but the people of nearby Tucson were terrified of living in close proximity to them and formed a mob that attacked them on 28 April 1871 in their camp. Many of the men were off hunting, so many of those killed were women and children and elderly men.

The Camp Grant incident incensed the rest of the Apaches and they were intent on revenge. The army was intent on ending the Apache threat and sent small forces, using scouts recruited from the reservation Apaches to hunt down the Indians in their homes, rewards being offered for the heads of important chiefs.

Salt Canyon

In the early 1870s General George Crook was sent to try to make peace with or subdue the Apaches. After the Battle of Salt Canyon, at which many Apaches were killed, many of them decided to seek peace, and even more did so after Crook's relentless campaign against them. On 27 April 1873 the last of the Apaches surrendered at Camp Verde.

Peace with the Apaches was not, however, permanent. There were complaints from the Apaches that the new army personnel were not so sympathetic as the previous army representatives had been and they complained of ill-treatment. These complaints were not unfounded, for in 1875 under a so-called consolidation policy they were forced into one overcrowded reservation at San Carlos instead of the spacious reservations that they had been promised. Also some of the Apaches had got bored and had broken free from the reservation area to pursue their old way of life, and this consolidation policy made more of them more determined to take this course of action.

Geronimo

The warrior Geronimo was one of these. He continued to harass the white men until he was captured by a trick in 1877 by John Philip Clum, the agent of the San Carlos reservation. He eventually escaped and the Apaches spent some years conducting raids on Mexican towns and villages and in attacking American ranches and settlements.

In 1882 General George Crook was recalled to Arizona and once again some of the Apaches from the reservations were used as scouts and interpreters to try to bring in their more warlike comrades. Crook waited until the Apaches made a raid from Mexico across the border into American territory. This meant that he was allowed to pursue them into Mexico and it was his intention to track the Apaches right to their own homes. He and his men set out in May 1883, travelling mainly at night. They captured Geronimo's camp and the women and children in it, the men being out on a raiding party at that time.

Crook invited Geronimo to talks. Eventually the Apaches were tired of being tracked down and agreed to engage in peace talks. Crook's terms seemed to be generous, and in February 1884 Geronimo and his fellow Apaches duly arrived in San Carlos which was under the control of General Crook.

There was relative peace for a while but the Apaches grew bored and missed their own way of life and there was quarrelling between the soldiers and the agents who were in charge of the reservation. The Apaches particularly missed their corn beer, or *tiswin*, which was prohibited in the reservations.

In May 1885 Geronimo and some of his people decided to make their escape, cutting the telegraph wires as they went. The Apaches succeeded in crossing the border to Mexico, back to their old haunts. With the help once again of Indian scouts they held peace talks with Geronimo and some of the rest of the Indian leaders. General Crook promised that they would be sent east for a few years and then be allowed back to Arizona.

Geronimo's surrender did not last long and, having obtained some spirits from a white trader, he and some of his people with a bit of Dutch courage broke camp and fled south. General Crook's superiors thought that he had been too lax with Geronimo and his people and he resigned.

General Nelson Miles took over the task of bringing in Geronimo, and he decided to adopt new tactics. Instead of using Indian scouts, he looked to the cavalry to perform the task of ending the Apaches' freedom. This did not prove an easy task and the Apaches continued their task of stealing cattle and killing settlers.

Peace and exile

In July 1886 Geronimo and his fellow-leader, Naches, decided
to surrender if the terms were to their liking. Lieutenant Charles
Gatewood was chosen to help conduct the peace talks because
he had served under General Crook and had experience of the
Apaches. Geronimo and the rest agreed to the peace terms and
they were sent by train to Florida into exile. The Apaches were
later removed to Mount Vernon Barracks in Alabama and later
to Fort Sill, Indian Territory.

See APACHE PASS; CAMP GRANT; CLUM, JOHN PHILIP; COCHISE;
CROOK, GENERAL GEORGE; GERONIMO; MANGAS COLORADAS; SALT
CANYON.

APACHE KID

The Apache Kid was a sergeant in the Apache government
scouts and a protégé of army scout Al Sieber until one day he
left the reservation at San Carlos intent on murdering an Indian
who had killed his father. His friend and mentor, Sieber, attempted to arrest him and the Apache Kid shot him in the leg
before fleeing from San Carlos. For the next few years the
Apache Kid lived the life of an outlaw, rustling cattle, holding
up wagon trains, murdering ranchers and abducting women
from reservations and then abandoning them.

He was much wanted by the authorities, and Sheriff Glen
Reynolds with his deputy captured the Kid and some other
wanted Apaches, but on the way to jail the Kid overpowered
Sheriff Reynolds. While he was trying to get free, one of the
other Apaches shot Reynolds dead. Posses soon caught the
Apache Kid's companions but the Kid himself was never seen
again by the white men.

APACHE PASS

The Apache Pass was the scene of an ambush attack by Apache

warriors under the leadership of Cochise and Mangas Coloradas on a party of Californian Volunteers under the leadership of Captain Thomas Roberts. There were several hundred more Apaches than there were Volunteers but Roberts had two mountain howitzer guns with his party. When these were trained on the Apaches they hastily withdrew, never having encountered shellfire before. Mangas Colorados was wounded in the chest as he retreated.

ARAPAHO INDIANS

The Arapaho migrated south and west until by 1790 they were on the central Great Plains. Having acquired horses from the Comanche, they became nomadic buffalo hunters, using the animals to provide food, clothing and housing.

Cheyenne

In the 1830s the Arapaho Indians divided into two branches, north and south. The southern Arapaho developed an association with the southern Cheyenne.

They had trouble with the American government when some of the Arapaho and some of the Comanche attacked wagon trains on the Santa Fe trail. In 1851 the Plains Indians, including the Arapaho, signed their first treaty with the American government, Washington recognizing the Indians' rights to the land and the Indians allowing the whites to build roads through it.

Fort Wise Treaty

Because of the decline in the number of buffalo, the Arapaho were worried about their survival. In 1858, in conjunction with other Plains Indians, the Arapaho indicated to the American government that they wished to live on certain lands and farm them, seeking help from the government in the form of protection by the army and farming tools. By the Fort Wise Treaty in 1861 the southern Arapaho and the southern Cheyenne gave up most of their land in return for a triangle of land around the edge of the Arkansas River and for annuities for fifteen years from the government. The Indians felt, however, that they had been short-changed and repudiated the terms of the treaty.

Relations between the Arapaho and Major-General Samuel Curtis, who was the army commander of the Kansas and Colorado Department, were strained. He was particularly anxious to rid the area of the Indian threat, and equally anxious to do so was Colonel John Chivington. On a suspicion of cattle raiding by the Cheyenne, Chivington attacked Cheyenne villages and one of his junior officers shot an Indian chief who came in peace. Naturally the Cheyenne and their friends, the Arapaho, were incensed and intent on revenge.

Denver

At a ranch outside Denver the members of a family named Hungate were murdered by the Cheyenne, abetted by some of the Arapaho. Further attacks by the Indians occurred and Denver was practically cut off from the rest of the country as all traffic on the trails was attacked. In order to relieve Denver, the American War Department was planning to raise a regiment of Indian volunteers who would serve for a hundred days under Chivington in order to bring to an end the Indian threat to peace.

Sand Creek

However, the Cheyennes were tired of war and sought peace, provided this was also accorded to the Arapaho and other tribes. The Indians thought that they had reached a deal with Major Edward Wynkoop at Fort Lyon. Chivington, intent on destroying the Indians, complained that Wynkoop was being too conciliatory to the Indians and had him replaced by Major Scott Anthony. The latter told Chief Black Kettle of the Cheyenne, who was representing the Cheyenne, the Arapaho and some other tribes, to move the Indians to a place called Sand Creek, an almost dry watercourse, supposedly to enable them to do some hunting.

In November 1864, Chivington and his men then approached the camp of the Cheyenne and the Arapaho and slaughtered the Indians who had been taking by surprise at night and who had already surrendered many of their weapons to the white men as part of their peace treaty. It was a terrible massacre and one that involved much mutilation, and some of Chivington's force refused to take part in it.

The Sand Creek massacre brought some of the northern Cheyenne and northern Arapaho, together with other tribes, to launch a combined attack in Colorado. Chivington was condemned by a military board but he was not punished since he had left the army.

The end of the Civil War
In April 1865 the Civil War came to an end and more people were free to turn their attention to the Indian question. This became increasingly important as the uniting of the east and the west of the country was now on the agenda and white migration west might be hindered by the presence of the Indians.

Sioux
America was intent on national expansion and the migration westward began with a vengeance. But the opening up of the West brought new problems for the Indians, as new roads were constructed to improve the passage of transport. They were not slow to show their opposition to this as they struggled to maintain their land, their animals and their identity. In this struggle much of the history of the Arapaho is the history of their allies, the Sioux.

Oklahoma
In 1867 the southern Arapaho and the southern Cheyenne were

assigned a reservation in what is now Oklahoma. They hoped to supplement the rations provided by the government by farming. Although they did not wish to abandon entirely their old way of life, they really had no choice because of the virtual extinction of the buffalo, which had been so central to their way of life. Meanwhile the northern Arapaho settled in a reservation in Wyoming.

In 1891 the southern Arapaho and Cheyenne sold their supposedly surplus land to the American government and many white settlers rushed to Oklahoma to occupy this land. The plains-roaming tribes were reduced to the confines of a reservation. *See* SIOUX.

ARIVAIPA APACHES *see* APACHES.

ARIZONA MARY

Arizona Mary was one of the new-style women that the opening up of the West created in America. Although many of the women involved in the West were working women who were employed in the traditional female jobs of cook, laundress, teacher, etc, not to mention prostitute, or were army wives, there were some women who worked alongside the men doing the same kind of work. Arizona Mary was one of this new breed and she guided her team of oxen dragging their freight down the wilderness trail with the best of the men.

ASTOR, JOHN JACOB

John Jacob Astor (1763–1848) was the founder of the American Fur Company (1808). Born in Germany, he went to New York at the age of twenty and found employment with a fur merchant. He set up on his own in the fur trade and made a fortune exporting furs to China, being regarded as one of the wealthiest men in America.

He next thought to monopolize the fur trade of Louisiana. In 1808 he formed the American Fur Company with the encouragement of Thomas Jefferson and in 1810 he created the Pacific Fur Company to handle the far west part of the fur business. The company was to have a headquarters at the mouth of the Columbia River and a series of forts stretching west to the Pacific coast.

Astor sent two expeditions to the Pacific. One of these went by sea and was led by Jonathan Thorne and the other went overland led by Wilson Price Hunt. Neither met with good fortune.

Tonquin

The sea journey, made on the *Tonquin*, was fraught with problems, largely because Thorne was such a tyrant that he almost caused a mutiny. When the ship arrived at the mouth of the Columbia, the sea was high and one of the ship's longboats sank and all the people in it were drowned. Eventually the survivors reached the shore in April 1811 and set about building a fort to be called Astoria, named after John Astor. While the fort was being built, the *Tonquin* sailed along the coast to trade with the Indians but this did not prove to be a good idea. Thorne is said to have insulted an Indian chief and the Indians attacked the ship and killed most of the crew. The survivors blew up the ship and the Indians who had boarded it. Opinions vary as to whether there were any survivors of this. Some sources indicate that there were a few who eventually made their way back.

Overland to the Pacific

Wilson Price Hunt was instructed to make his way with his party from St Louis, Missouri, to Yellowstone. The party was then to cross the Rockies and join forces with Thorne on the Pacific coast. Because of potential danger from the Blackfeet Indians, they changed their route for one that proceeded due west. They crossed the Big Horn River and reached the Snake

River. They exchanged their horses for canoes with some Indians and intended going down the river until they reached the mountains. Unfortunately the river became unnavigable and many of the canoes sank, with some loss of life and much loss of provisions.

Hunt's party divided into groups to cross the Cascade Mountains, but severe cold and intense snow hindered progress and some men died and some deserted. The groups took a long time to reach Fort Astoria, the first group arriving in January 1812 and Hunt's group arriving in February. A supply ship arrived and things began to look more optimistic but then in June 1812 America and Britain went to war and, mindful of the superiority of British sea power, the inhabitants of Fort Astoria sold out to traders from the North West Company. This particular dream of Astor's had failed.

However, this setback did not deter him. Astor established a virtual monopoly on fur trading around the Great Lakes and went on to establish the western division of the American Fur Company, which demolished its competitors. At first the American Fur Company, or the Company as it was known, confined its business to the Missouri and its tributaries but then in 1831 it turned its business interests to the Green and Wind Rivers of Wyoming. Here it engaged in rivalry with the Rocky Mountain Fur Company, which sold out to Astor in 1834.

Later the same year Astor sold his shares in the American Fur Company and retired. He had observed that silk and not beaver was now being favoured by the hat industry in Europe and America. Up until then the underfur of the beaver had been much used in men's hats. The beaver fur trade virtually came to an end in 1840, by which time the price of beaver pelts had dropped by a huge margin. Astor had got out at the right time and is said to have made profits of twenty million dollars

See FUR TRADE.

AUSTIN, STEPHEN

Stephen Austin was one of the first Americans to settle in Texas. He was the eldest son of Moses Austin, who, having suffered financial setbacks in Missouri, decided to go to Texas. However, Moses fell ill on the journey and caught pneumonia and died. His dying wish requested that his son Stephen go on to Texas as he himself had intended to do.

AUTRY, GENE

Gene Autry (1907–) is famous for his appearances as a film actor and singer in many western films. Born in Texas, his own background was based in the west and his father was a cattle-dealer and horse-trader.

He started his career off as a singer but soon turned to films, and the film *In Old Santa Fe* (1934) marked the start of what was to be a long film singing career. In this was also George 'Gabby' Hayes, who was to become famous as Autry's side-kick. Other sidekicks included Smiley Burnette and Pat Buttram. Autry's horse, Champion, also became famous.

Autry's films usually included music, comedy and romance as well as fights and horseback pursuits. He used his role as a screen cowboy to try to instil moral values in people. He was behind the 'Ten Commandments of the Cowboy', which laid down the basic moral requirements of a cowboy. These included never taking unfair advantage of other people, never betraying a trust, always keeping his word, always telling the truth, always being kind to children, old people and animals, always showing tolerance, always helping people in distress, always working hard, always respecting women, his parents and the law, always being clean in thought, speech and habits and always being patriotic.

During the 1940s Autry was a rodeo producer. He did much to change the rodeo scene, bringing in singers and other entertainers as well as the rodeo contestants and thereby making rodeo entertainment more general.

Autry enlisted in the Army Air Corps in 1942 during World War II, thereby living up to his tenet that cowboys should be patriotic. His action was admirable but it left the way open for Roy Rogers to take over Autry's role as 'King of the Cowboys'. Autry turned to business as well as films and became a multi-millionaire. In 1960 he and Champion retired from film appearances. *See* ROY ROGERS.

AVERILL, JIM

Jim Averill was a victim of the struggle between the cattle barons of Wyoming and the homesteaders. The cattle barons, who laid claim to what had once been public ranges, objected to the increase in the number of homesteaders in the area, especially after the Homestead Act of 1862, which was passed to promote settlement in the West. The cattle barons accused the homesteaders of stealing their cattle from the ranges and rebranding the cattle, while the homesteaders accused the cattle barons or stockmen of illegally taking the best grassland for themselves. In order to protect their herds from rustlers, the stockmen employed range detectives, many of them posing as ordinary cowhands, to detect and report cases of stock theft and rebranding. Despite this, rustling continued.

Jim Averill was the owner of a store and a saloon and the business partner of Ella Watson in Sweetwater County. Ella purchased a small ranch beside the saloon and is said to have stocked it with steers, possibly rustled, given to her by cowboys in exchange for her sexual favours. Meanwhile her business partner, Jim Averill, was avidly denouncing the actions of the cattle barons and their range detectives in the pages of the *Casper Weekly Mail*.

Both of them paid a terrible price for their crossing of the stockmen. They were both warned that it was in their interests to get out of the area but both refused. Following this refusal, in July 1889, they were subjected to an attack by a lynch mob that, without even going through the motions of a trial, strung them up to die on a nearby tree. It was widely believed that a stockman called Albert Bothwell was behind the lynchings but no indictments in connection with the crime were ever made. The reputation of Ella Watson was blackened. She was depicted as a notorious cattle rustler and given the nickname 'Cattle Kate'.

The hangings of Jim Averill and Ella Watson were just the start of a relentless campaign organized by the stockmen. From them on violence spread and lynching followed lynching.

B

BILLY THE KID

Billy the Kid (1859–91) was born Henry McCarty into a slum area of New York occupied mainly by Irish immigrants. During the Civil War the family moved to Kansas and his father died in Coffeyville. His mother suffered from tuberculosis and moved to the healthier climate of Colorado. Her second husband was William Henry Antrim, a prospector and a bartender.

The Antrim family lived in a log cabin in the mining settlement of Silver City. Billy's mother died of her tubercular infection when Billy was fourteen and he started to have behavioural problems. At fifteen he became a fugitive from justice when he escaped from jail after stealing some washing from a laundry.

He went to Mount Graham, Arizona, where he found work as a teamster and cowboy. Feeling that because of his youth he was not getting proper men's work, he turned to cattle-rustling and horse-thieving. He also learned to handle a gun with dexterity.

In March 1876 he was imprisoned in Camp Grant for stealing a horse belonging to a cavalry sergeant. He succeeded in escaping but returned to the Camp Grant area not long afterwards, dressed extremely stylishly. In August 1877 he killed a man called Windy Cahill who was teasing him and with whom he had been playing cards. The Kid was arrested and sent to await trial but once again he escaped.

Lincoln County War

He then went back to New Mexico and began calling himself William Bonney. While there he took part in the Lincoln County War. He worked as a ranch-hand for Tunstall and became part of his gang against Chisum. Tunstall was held in very high regard by him and he was extremely upset by his death. He swore vengeance on anyone who had been connected with it. The story of this is told in the entry on the Lincoln County War.

Death

Pat Garrett was relentless in his pursuit of Billy the Kid and finally tracked him down to a friend's house on the night of 14 July 1881. There he shot him dead. Billy the Kid was only twenty-one when he died.

Billy the Kid was small, lithe and wiry. He became notorious as a gunman and is one of the best known of the figures in the legend of the West. As is the case with several of the figures who feature in this legend, some of the information that has been circulated about Billy the Kid is thought to have been fictitious or highly exaggerated. In particular, the true tally of his killings is thought to be six, although various colourful estimates place it far beyond this. *See* LINCOLN COUNTY WAR.

BLACK KETTLE

Black Kettle is remembered in the history of the West as the Cheyenne chief who was in charge of a group of his own men

and some Arapaho and members of other Indian tribes when
they were sent by Major Scott Anthony to Sand Creek. This was
supposedly a safe place where they would be able to hunt and be
protected by the army. In fact it was Anthony's intention to massacre them there, and this was done by troops under the command of Colonel Chivington. The story of this terrible slaughter
is told under the entry on the Arapaho in the section on Sand
Creek.

Peace of Medicine Lodge Creek
Black Kettle was one of the few who escaped. For some time
then he and members of his tribe, along with members of the
Arapaho tribe, harassed the white settlers and had skirmishes
with army forces but eventually in October 1867 a peace was
agreed between the white men and the central and southern Indian tribes at Medicine Lodge Creek in Kansas. Some Indian
chiefs refused to sign the peace agreement but Black Kettle did.
War continued between the whites and some of the Indians.

Black Kettle had difficulty in obtaining the arms and ammunition promised to his people under the terms of the peace
agreement for the annual buffalo hunt, but eventually these
were supplied in August 1868. After the hunt he and his people
established their winter quarters by the Washita River, as they
had been directed to by the terms of the peace agreement. They
thought that they were safe but they were wrong.

Washita
Colonel George Armstrong Custer, acting on orders from General Philip Sheridan, appeared with the Seventh Cavalry and attacked the Cheyenne settlement. Many of the people there were
women, children and old men. A few Indians escaped but many
of them were killed and a few were taken prisoner. The settlement was burned and the horses destroyed. It had been an un-
provoked attack on a peaceful settlement.

Black Kettle tried to escape on horseback with his wife. However, he was shot as he rode away, and he and his wife both died.

The intention of the authorities had been to put an end to the raids that were still going on in the area and indeed Black Kettle is thought to have had some active warriors in his camp, although he announced himself to be in favour of peace. Still, it was a terrible massacre and one that was to incense the Indians. *See* ARAPAHO.

BLUE, TEDDY *see* ABBOTT, EDWARD C.

BONNEY, WILLIAM
William Bonney was an alias adopted by Billy the Kid. *See* BILLY THE KID.

BOONE, DANIEL
Daniel Boone (1734–1820) is regarded by many as the epitome of the frontiersman. Born into a Quaker family in Pennsylvania, Boone and his family moved to the Yadkin Valley of North Carolina. There he learned to farm and hunt and there he married Rebecca Brian. There, too, he learned a great deal about wild life and how to survive in the wilderness from the Indians. For a time he fought in the Seven Years' War.

In the winter of 1767, having heard much about Kentucky from his brother-in-law, John Stewart, he made a trip there, followed by other trips between 1769 and 1771. He and some other hunters passed through the Cumberland Gap and built a shelter at Station Camp Creek. They then separated to explore the wilderness, Boone going as far north as the Ohio River.

He was determined to move his family to Kentucky but an attempt to do so in 1773 failed tragically. The family were attacked by Indians and the eldest son was killed. This did not deter Boone from his plan to settle in Kentucky, and in 1775 he led a party through the Cumberland Gap and with them cleared a trail to the Kentucky River, which became known as the Wilderness Road. On the south bank of the river they built a settlement and named it Boonesborough. Meanwhile Boone's friend, Judge Richard Henderson, had bought a piece of land stretching from the Kentucky River to an area south of the Cumberland Gap from the Cherokee Indians.

During the American War of Independence with Britain, Boone was involved in directing the defence of the frontier settlements against attacks by the British and by the local Indians. He and a party set out in 1778 to get some salt from the spring at Blue Licks and were captured by the Shawnee, who held them hostage and practically adopted them, so impressed were they by their courage.

On hearing that the Shawnee were planning a raid on Boonesborough, Boone succeeded in escaping and ran 160 miles through the forest to warn the fort. This feat took him four days and his warning was in time. The Shawnee arrived and mounted a siege but the holders of the fort withstood it.

Later Boone was charged with treason for having dealings with the Shawnee and with the British but he was acquitted. Throughout his life he acquired a good deal of land but lost most of it for various reasons, some of them legal snags. In particular he was given a large tract of Louisiana while it belonged to Spain and lost it when Spain sold it all to France. He died at the age of eighty-five in Missouri.

Boone acquired a reputation as an Indian-fighter, although in fact it is thought that he killed only one Indian during his lifetime and he had had very good relations with the local Indians in his youth. His prowess as an Indian fighter became greatly exaggerated both during his lifetime and afterwards. He was noted for his excellent frontier skills but these again have been greatly exaggerated.

In the story of the West he is remembered as being the first trailblazer of America's progress west. As such he has acquired a reputation of grossly exaggerated importance.

BOZEMAN TRAIL

The Bozeman Trail is principally remembered in the history of the West for its connection with the struggle between the Sioux Indians and the white men. The Bozeman Trail gave access to the goldfields of Montana and ran through Powder River country, land that was dear to the Sioux because not only was it their land but it was one of the few surviving buffalo ranges. The authorities' decision to build forts along the trail to provide protection from the Sioux angered the great warrior chief Red Cloud and led to war. This is dealt with in the article on Red Cloud. *See* RED CLOUD.

BRIDGER, JIM

Jim Bridger (1804–81) was a fur trapper who was one of the first mountain men, a trapper who was not a permanent employee of a fur company. Born in Virginia, he moved to St Louis and worked there as a blacksmith. In 1822 he took up an offer made by William Ashley and Andrew Henry to take self-employed trappers into the wilderness, leave them to their work and later meet them at a set meeting place where they would pay them for their catch. This saved them building trading posts, which were much disliked by the Indians who saw them as an indication of white occupation and supremacy. The enterprise became the Rocky Mountain Fur Company, which was bought in 1834 by Astor, owner of the American Fur Company.

Bridger, like many other mountain men, married an Indian wife—in fact he married three, surviving all of them. He has become one of the legendary figures of the West with a good deal of fiction attached to him. This was partly because he was a teller of tall tales—told orally because he could neither read nor write.

He is, however, generally credited with the discovery of the Great Salt Lake. He is thought to have discovered it when he took a canoe down the dangerous Bear River to settle a bet about where it flowed.

As well as being a trapper, Bridger had other jobs. Particularly after the decline of the beaver industry, Bridger was an army scout, expedition guide and Indian-fighter. He is said to have had extremely good mapping skills and to have been fluent in Spanish and French. Fort Bridger on the Oregon Trail was built by him as a trading post. It was destroyed by in an attack by Mormons complaining about the extortionate prices on their trek west.

In 1865 he helped to blaze the Bozeman Trail from Nebraska to Montana to facilitate the goldrush prospectors. He was adviser to Colonel Carrington in his campaign against the Sioux under Red Cloud before he retired because of failing eyesight. He died at the age of seventy-seven.

BUFFALO BILL *see* CODY, WILLIAM.

C

CALAMITY JANE

Calamity Jane (?–1903), whose real name was Martha Jane Cannary, although some sources give the surname as Canary or Canarray, was born in Missouri probably somewhere between 1844 and 1852, the exact date of her birth not having been established. She is one of the legendary figures of the West and much of the information disseminated about her is fictitious or exaggerated, it being difficult to separate the two.

It is said that a great deal of the fiction about her was started by herself and she is thought to have been a notorious liar. She claimed, for example, to be the lover, or even the wife of, Wild Bill Hickok, which is thought to be extremely unlikely, although she may well have met him at Deadwood. She also claimed to have been an army scout, an Indian fighter, a rider for Pony Express and a wagon freighter.

Few things are known about her for certain. We know that she frequently wore male dress, was given to drinking too much and to brawling and swearing and that she was a good shot. It is thought likely that she worked as a prostitute, especially towards the end of her life, and that she worked bravely as a nurse during an outbreak of smallpox in Dakota during the 1870s.

She died in 1903 in South Dakota. She had expressed a wish to be buried next to Wild Bill Hickok and her wish was granted.

Hollywood capitalized on this larger than life legend. Perhaps the most famous screen Calamity Jane was Doris Day who appeared in a musical version of the story.

CARSON, KIT

Kit Carson (1809–68), whose full name was Christopher Houston Carson, was a mountain man, a trapper and fur trader who worked for himself rather than for a company, and a scout who has become one of the great legendary figures of the West. He is chiefly remembered as the scout and guide for John Fremont on his map-making expeditions in the 1840s.

Fremont was very impressed by Carson and wrote glowing reports of him. Because of this, he became a legend and many books were written with Carson as their hero. His fictional adventures were even more spectacular than his actual ones.

Mountain man

At the age of sixteen, Carson, who was very small for his age, was working with a saddler in Franklin, Missouri, when he left secretly to join a wagon train that was leaving for Santa Fe, then part of Mexico. He became a trapper in the southern Rocky Mountains. Like many mountain men, he was friendly with some of the Indian peoples and an enemy of others. He fought with the Apache and Comanche but was helpful to the Cheyenne.

Many mountain men married Indian women and Carson was one of them. First he married the daughter of an Arapaho chief but she died after giving birth to a daughter. He then married a Cheyenne woman who divorced him.

By the end of the 1830s the heyday of the trade in beaver fur was over. The underfur of beaver had been much used in the making of men's hats but now silk was in fashion. Carson, like other trappers, was in need of other work. It was at this point that he became a scout and guide for Fremont.

Navaho
After scouting for the army during the Mexican War, he farmed for a while and served as an Indian agent. Carson received an army commission at the start of the Civil War. Given the rank of colonel, in 1863 he was ordered by General James Carleton to take charge of a volunteer force to subdue the Navaho. The story of this is told in the entry at Navaho but basically Carson subdued them by starving the Navaho, stealing or killing their sheep and burning their homes.

Obviously the Navaho had no cause to love Carson. However, the Ute tribe had occasion to be grateful to him, since he urged the government to keep the promises that had been made to the Indians.

Carson rose to the rank of brigadier-general in the army. He died in 1868 when he was nearly sixty years old. *See* FREMONT, JOHN and NAVAHO.

CASSIDY, BUTCH
Butch Cassidy (1866–1911?) is the name by which Robert LeRoy Parker is better known. He was born in Utah to a Mor-

mon family. He was raised on a ranch and struck up a great friendship with a cowboy turned cattle-rustler called Mike Cassidy. He left home at sixteen to join Cassidy, adopted Cassidy's surname and turned to a life of cattle-rustling and other crimes, such as horse-stealing, bank robbery and train hold-ups. Parker is thought to have acquired the name 'Butch' because he once worked in a butcher's shop.

The Wild Bunch and the Sundance Kid

He was arrested for cattle-stealing in Wyoming in 1894 and spent two years in the Wyoming State Penitentiary. After he was released he became the leader of the gang known as the Wild Bunch, one of the members of which was the Sundance Kid, properly called Harry Longabaugh, who was a particular friend of Butch Cassidy. Members of the gang varied a bit from time to time but outlaws who were at some point members of the Wild Bunch include Bill Carver, Ben Kilpatrick, Harvey Logan, known as 'Kid Curry', Harry Tracy, and others.

The gang operated out of a valley in north Wyoming, known as the Hole in the Wall, being so called because of a gash in the rock that acted as a narrow entrance. Because it was near good grazing country it was an excellent area for cattle-rustlers and because it was so isolated it was a natural hideout for outlaws.

The Wild Bunch held up the mining camp at Castle Gate, Utah, in April 1897 and went on to a series of other raids and hold-ups. They executed a number of train hold-ups, particularly of trains belonging to the Union Pacific. After such a hold-up at Tipton, Wyoming, in August 1900, the Union Pacific organized a detective force, complete with its own train, to track down the members of the Wild Bunch. The force and the train were kept in readiness to be dispatched to wherever the gang struck. The gang did strike—at a Great Northern Railroad train in Montana in July 1901 but they escaped.

The leaving of North America

Butch Cassidy decided that things were getting a little too hot, with the Pinkerton Detective Agency, lawmen and the detectives of the Union Pacific all in pursuit of the members of the gang. Besides, the telephone and telegraph systems were making it easier to track down the lawless.

He and the Sundance Kid, accompanied by the Sundance Kid's mistress, Etta Place, decided to leave the gang and also to leave America in 1902. There are various theories as to where they went but they ended up in South America, perhaps going to Brazil, perhaps to Chile or the Argentine. Etta Place, being unwell, was escorted back to the United States in 1907 by the Sundance Kid and he returned on his own some time later.

Butch Cassidy and the Sundance Kid are then thought to have moved to Bolivia and to have undertaken a few bank robberies, although the scale of their crimes in South America is said to have been small. What happened after that has been the subject of much speculation.

Likely fates

A common story is that Cassidy and his friend were killed by Bolivian soldiers, but the sister of Butch Cassidy claimed that her brother escaped from the soldiers and returned to the United States to live in obscurity, paying her a surprise visit in 1929. Yet another story has it that Cassidy returned to the States, having changed his appearance and changed his name to William Thadeus Phillips, and set up a business in Iowa.

The Sundance Kid, according to some sources, also returned and married Etta. This, however, is speculation rather than fact.

The uncertainty about what happened to them has simply added to the status of the two friends as part of the legend of the West. As with other similar figures, history has tended to romanticize them and their exploits have been exaggerated.

CHEYENNE

The Cheyenne Indians were frequently allies of the Arapaho. They were together at the terrible massacre of Sand Creek, which is dealt with in the article at Arapaho. *See* ARAPAHO.

CHISUM, JOHN

John Chisum (1824–84) was a rancher who played a major part in the events relating to the Lincoln County War. *See* LINCOLN COUNTY WAR.

CLANTONS, THE

The Clanton family is remembered in the history of the West because some of its members comprised the other party in the gunfight at the OK Corral in Tombstone, Arizona, the more prominent party being Wyatt Earp's party. The Clanton family consisted of N. H. ('Old Man') Clanton and his sons, Billy, Ike and Phineas, and with some friends, including Frank and Tom McLaury, they formed a gang known as the Cowboys. The details of the Earp-Clanton confrontation are given under Wyatt Earp at the section entitled OK Corral. *See* EARP, WYATT.

CLARK, WILLIAM

William Clark was one of the leaders of the Lewis and Clark expedition. *See* LEWIS AND CLARK EXPEDITION.

COCHISE

Cochise was the son-in-law of Mangas Colorados, a chief of the Chiricahua tribe of the Apaches. He was himself a great warrior chief of the Chiricahua. *See* APACHE.

CODY, WILLIAM FREDERICK

William Cody (1846–1917) is better known as Buffalo Bill and is remembered as one of the sharpshooters of the West. He owes his nickname to the fact that he shot a great many buffalo for the Kansas Pacific Railroad in 1867–68, the meat of the buffalo being used to feed the railroad crews and the hides being used to make machine belts in the east.

He was born in Iowa but his family moved to Kansas in 1854. His father died in 1857 and the young William was left to support the family. By the time he was fourteen, he had worked as a Pony Express rider, a prospector, a drover and a trapper. He served in the Civil War with irregular militia units and with the Seventh Kansas Volunteer Cavalry, his wartime duties including scouting and spying.

After the war he ran an inn for a time with the woman whom he had married in 1866, Louisa Frederici. He soon tired of this and went farther west to act as a guide, scout and buffalo hunter. It was then that he worked for the Kansas-Pacific Railroad, killing buffalo.

Cody then served in the cavalry from 1868. He worked as a scout and fought in several campaigns against the Indians. Then he began escorting hunting parties for wealthy men on the transcontinental railroad.

Buntline

The dime novelist Ned Buntline wrote stories about him and created the legend about him. In 1872 he appeared in Buntline's melodrama, *The Scouts of the Prairie*. Critics slated it but audiences appeared to love it. Cody toured with the show for a while but occasionally had to leave to go and scout for the army in wars against the Indians.

Wild West Show

Cody's popular success in the stage show led him to organize an extravaganza, called an *Old Glory Blowout*, in 1882 in North Platte, Nebraska, to celebrate 4 July. This show included shooting contests and roping and riding contests for cowboys and was the forerunner of the first Wild West Show, which he organized at Omaha Fair Grounds, 19 May 1883. This included Cody and other marksmen, an exhibition of cowboy skills, a mock attack on the Deadwood Stage, a mock battle depicting the capture and death of a scout by savages, and a mock hunt with buffalo, elk, deer, wild horses, etc.

The show was a huge success and toured for many years. Cody constantly added to the range and variety of acts, some incorporating real-life characters and events in the history of the West. Annie Oakley's marksman tricks were an important part of the show, which later toured Britain and parts of Europe.

COW TOWNS

The cow towns of Kansas were boom towns that owed their prosperity to their proximity to a railroad and a cattle trail. They were thus the points at which cattle arrived along the trail from the west and were shipped off to the east. Cow towns, although noted for their affluence, were also notorious for trouble. Stockmen bought and sold cattle, cowboys were looking for ways to spend their money after weeks on a lonely trail, land speculators were out to make a profit and soldiers from the frontier posts added to the troublesome mixture.

Leisure facilities included saloons, which provided hard liquor, and gambling and houses of prostitution. Tempers were apt to run high and gunfights were common. To add to the problem, it was frequently difficult to get lawmen to control towns in which there was such a high level of violence and lawlessness. Because of this, it was quite common for people who had themselves led violent, lawless lives to become official lawmen.

A notable feature of the Kansas cow towns was that their boom time did not last long. As one cow town faded in importance, another took its place, usually because the railroad had pushed on. *See* ABILENE; DODGE CITY; ELLSWORTH and WICHITA.

CRAZY HORSE

Crazy Horse (1841–77) was a Sioux warrior who was noted for

his fearlessness and his strangeness. Going into battle naked but for a loin cloth, he struck terror into the hearts of his enemies. He was in charge of a decoy party when Red Cloud organized the Fetterman Massacre (1866) at Lodge Trail Ridge when the Sioux annihilated a party of troops under the command of William Judd Fetterman, who was fooled into believing that there were far fewer Indians against him than there were. This is dealt with in the entry on Red Cloud.

Crazy Horse became chief of the Oglala Sioux and became powerful among the Sioux generally. Both before and after, he took part in many skirmishes and battles against the white men, for whom he is said to have had a bitter hatred. His intention was to prevent settlers from occupying Sioux lands and specifically to prevent them from building a second transcontinental railroad.

The Battle of Little Bighorn

He is particularly noted as one of the Indian leaders at one of the most legendary confrontations in the West. This took place near the Little Bighorn River in Montana on 25 June 1876. The confrontation was between a large combined force of Sioux and northern Cheyenne and the Seventh Cavalry under the command of Colonel George Armstrong Custer. There was also an infantry troop under the command of Colonel John Gibbon taking part in the conflict, the idea being that the Indians would be trapped between the cavalry and the infantry.

Custer moved his men on at a great pace to catch up with the Indians. Seeing an Indian encampment, he ignored his own Indian scouts' advice, which was that he should wait for reinforcements, given the number of Indians assembled there, possibly the greatest single force of Indians ever gathered together.

He decided to divide his regiment in order to mount a successful attack and prevent the Indians from escaping. One section was sent under the command of Captain Frederick Benteen to the hills on the south. A force under Major Marcus Reno was ordered to cross the Little Bighorn River and attack the Indian settlement from the south, the rest of the regiment being ordered to proceed in a direction parallel to Reno to support the action of his force.

Custer, however, had changed his mind and the rest of the regiment was not there to support Reno when he attacked the settlement. He had moved north, it is thought, with the intention of attacking the Indian settlement through a gap in the hills. However, Custer was never to reach the settlement.

Custer's Last Stand

His force was attacked from the first by a force of Huncpapa Sioux under the leadership of Chief Gall and then from the other side by a force of the Oglala Sioux led by Crazy Horse. Custer's men fought bravely but in vain. Not one was left alive. It was one of the great disasters of American military history and is popularly known as Custer's Last Stand. Because of it, both Custer and Crazy Horse earned a place in the legend of the West.

The American nation was incensed at this disaster. Everyone with any experience in fighting the Indians was dispatched to harass the Indians of the northern plains. All the reservations there were placed under military command and a law was passed forcing the Sioux to hand over their lands to the whites and to go to live on the reservations.

Death of Crazy Horse

Eventually in May 1877 Crazy Horse led his men into Fort Robinson, Nebraska, and surrendered. In September he was taken under guard to the military compound at Fort Robinson to be imprisoned, because he was regarded as being so dangerous. Realizing that he was about to be made a prisoner, Crazy Horse tried to escape and was stabbed with a bayonet by a soldier named William Gentle. He died shortly afterwards of the wound. *See* RED CLOUD and SIOUX.

CROCKETT, DAVY

Davy Crockett (1786–1836) is remembered in American history as one of the brave men who fought at the siege of the Alamo, which took place in 1836 in the Mexican War, and lost their lives in the process. He is also remembered as an early legendary figure of the West, being regarded by many as the epitome of the frontiersman.

In particular he is associated with hunting prowess. However, many tales relating to this are undoubtedly fictitious because Crockett was a noted teller of tall tales. A well known one relates to racoons. Crockett claimed that he did not have to use weapons to get rid of them, that he could get one of them to come from the highest of trees by simply grinning at them. *See* ALAMO.

CUSTER, COLONEL GEORGE ARMSTRONG

George Armstrong Custer (1839–76) is remembered in the legend of the West because of the disastrous battle that became known as Custer's Last Stand. He was in command of the Seventh Cavalry when it was completely routed by a force of Indians, many of them Sioux, at the Battle of Little Bighorn. The battle, which took place in June 1876, is described at the entry on Crazy Horse, who was one of the main Indian warrior chiefs who took part in the battle. Custer, who was known to the Indians as Long Hair, was killed in the battle, as were all the white men who took part in it.

Custer was a major-general in the Civil War but was reduced to the rank of captain after the war, eventually working himself back up to the rank of colonel. He and his men are remembered

for their bravery in their stance against the Indians at Little Bighorn, but he is thought to have been a poor commander and to
have made several military mistakes, perhaps because he was
too eager to seek glory. He is also said to have been moody and
often to have treated his men badly. At one point he had deserted his post to join his wife and had been court-martialled for
this (1867).

The battle at Little Bighorn is not the only incident involving
Indians for which Custer is remembered. He was in charge of
the Seventh Cavalry when it attacked Black Kettle's settlement
at Washita. The chief of the Cheyenne and many Indians, most
of them women, children and old men, were killed in what was
an unexpected attack on their winter quarters. The story of this
attack is told at the entry on Black Kettle. *See* BLACK KETTLE,
CRAZY HORSE.

D

DALTONS, THE

The Dalton brothers, Bob, Bill, Emmett and Grat, were part of a
large family who lived in Coffeyville in southern Kansas, the
Dalton family being relatives of the notorious Youngers. Another brother, Frank, was a deputy marshal who was shot and
killed when trying to arrest three whisky pedlars in Indian Territory. Of the four best-known Dalton brothers, Bob and Grat
both originally became lawmen, Emmett worked as a ranch-
hand and Bill got married and ostensibly settled down but this
respectability was not to last.

Bob and Grat became involved in getting rid of stolen livestock and in horse-stealing. After that they decided to turn their

hand to train robbery, Bill by this time having joined them. A great deal of the trouble that they caused was in Indian Territory but eventually they decided to become bank robbers in their home town of Coffeyville. Indeed, they decided to rob two banks at once.

Bob, Grat and Emmett, but not Bill, were part of the gang planning the bank robberies, as were Bill Powers and Dick Broadwell. On 5 October 1892 they decided to carry out their planned robberies.

Luck was not on their side, as the street between the two banks was under repair and they had to leave their horses quite a way from the banks. They were wearing rather ludicrous disguises of false moustaches and beards, and Bob and Emmett were recognized by a passer-by when they were taking around $20,000 from the First National Bank. The said passer-by raised the alarm and the men of the town hastily armed themselves to go in pursuit of the Daltons.

Meanwhile at the other bank across the street, the Condon Bank, the teller told the would-be robbers that the bank's safe had a tie-lock which could not be opened. This delay gave the men of the town time to catch up with the Dalton brothers and their accomplices. As the robbers tried to reach their horses, a gun battle broke out between them and the townsmen.

The result of the battle was that Bob and Grat were killed, as were their accomplices and four of the townsmen. Emmett survived and was given life imprisonment but was pardoned fourteen years later and went to California. He became an adviser to the makers of western films in Hollywood, one of which was entitled *The Last Stand of the Dalton Boys* (1912) and wrote books on law and order. He died in 1937 of natural causes.

Another member of the Dalton gang was Bill Doolin. He, however, was fortunate enough not to have taken part in the Coffeyville raids. *See* DOOLIN, BILL.

DIXON, MAYNARD

Maynard Dixon (1875-1946) was an artist who painted cowboy scenes. After studying art in San Francisco he worked in the southwest as a cowboy and so he had some idea of what the life of a cowboy involved. He painted murals and supplied illustrations for magazines. His depiction of the cowboy was rather stylized but also had authentic touches.

DODGE CITY

Dodge City was one of the Kansas cow towns that were brought to brief fame by the cattle industry. Before the arrival of the cattle industry in Dodge City, the buffalo trade had been its main business interest, and the route north from Texas taken by the buffalo hunters, Ed Jones and Jo Plumer, to the town provided the makings of a ready-made trail. In time the trail became extended, becoming known as the Western Trail.

As Wichita declined as a cow town around 1877, Dodge City started to boom. This boom, however, did not last, although by the standards of the other cow towns, it was long-lasting. By 1884 it was more or less over, the cattle industry being no longer of such importance to the town.

In its heyday Dodge City saw much wealth, as did the other cow towns of Kansas, but it also experienced the same disadvantages. A great deal of gambling, drinking, prostitution, fighting, shooting and general lawlessness went on. Indeed, as a result of its reputation, Dodge City became known as the 'Gomorrah of the Plains'.

Various lawmen were brought in to try to bring law and order to Dodge City. These included Bill Tilghman and Bat Masterson as well as the famous Wyatt Earp.

Dodge City lays claim to being the first town to have an area known as Boot Hill, although other towns were also to have areas so named. Boot Hill was in fact a burial ground, many men

being buried there after gunfights still with their boots on. *See*
EARP, WYATT; MASTERSON, BAT; and TILGHMAN, BILL.

DOOLIN, BILL

Known as the King of the Oklahoma Outlaws, Bill Doolin was
an Arkansas farm-hand who became a member of the Dalton
brothers' gang. He did not take part in the abortive raid on the
Coffeyville banks, supposedly because his horse went lame
when he was approaching the town, and thus did not die with
the other gang members.

After the deaths of Bob and Grat Dalton, Doolin organized
his own gang in Oklahoma Territory and was a good deal better
at planning robberies than the Daltons. Occasionally Bill
Dalton, who had also been absent from the Coffeyville bank
raids, joined in with the activities of Doolin's gang.

Oklahombres

For four years Doolin led his gang, known as the Oklahombres,
on a series of armed raids on trains and banks. The members of
the gang were excellent shots, had a good knowledge of the
Oklahoma Territory and had a safe hideout by the Cimarron
River. The townspeople of the Territory were quite well disposed towards Doolin, particularly the townspeople of the town
of Ingalls where Doolin had met and married a Methodist's
preacher's daughter. One of the reasons for Doolin's popularity
is his supposed generosity, even although he was being generous with other people's money.

The Doolin gang, then, had quite a lot going for them but the
law was after them. In order to speed up the taking of Doolin,
the railways and banks put up a reward of $5,000 for his cap-
ture.

A narrow escape

A lawman named Bill Tilghman actually stumbled accidentally

on the gang's hideout in January 1895, the outlaws being out of sight at the time. He is said to have seen the half-hidden guns trained on him but wisely decided to do nothing about it, he being alone at the time. Legend has it that Doolin refused to let his men shoot a man of Tilghman's calibre in the back but a more likely explanation is that Doolin knew that, if the popular lawman was shot, there would soon be a large posse sent out after them. By the time Tilghman returned with more men, Doolin and his gang had gone.

Arrest

Luck was beginning to run out for the Doolin gang. First, Bill Raidler, after a gunfight with Tilghman, was jailed for ten years in the Ohio Penitentiary, and then Bill Dalton and Red Weightman were both killed while resisting arrest. Then in December 1895 Tilghman caught up with Doolin in Eureka Springs in Arkansas where the outlaw was receiving treatment for rheumatism. Doolin was in the bathhouse and Tilghman entered it in disguise, as though himself taking a bath, and arrested Doolin at gunpoint. Doolin surrendered rather than be killed.

Escape and death

Doolin was taken for trial to Guthrie in Oklahoma and thousands gathered to see him at the station. He pleaded not guilty and was put in Guthrie jail to await trial. He escaped some months later, freeing several other prisoners as well.

It seems likely at that point that Doolin had decided to leave both the Territory and outlawry. Certainly he had packed his possessions in a wagon and was said to have made plans to move his wife and son with him out of the area, perhaps to Mexico, New Mexico or Canada. But his plans for a new life were not to be.

Somehow a lawman called Heck Thomas got to know that the Doolin family were hiding out in a farmhouse near Lawson and that they were planning to leave. Thomas and a posse rode out to the farmhouse to arrest Doolin but he resisted arrest and was shot by Thomas.

DUDE RANCH

A dude ranch is a ranch in which the owners take guests who live informally as part of the family and who are offered the opportunity to take part in various outdoor pursuits connected with life on a ranch. These include ranch-work, horse-riding, hunting, fishing, hiking and so on. Although dude ranch holidays are a thriving part of the modern American vacation scene, the dude ranch has been popular in the west for quite some time.

The term first appeared in the 1870s. Visitors to the West were attracted by the beauty of the scenery and perhaps by the prospect of hunting parties. A stay on a dude ranch allowed people to get a taste of life in the Wild West without experiencing the hardships that could be associated with such a life.

Travel west became more attractive when access was greatly improved by the extension of the railroad westwards. There were dude ranches in Colorado in the 1870s and in Wyoming in the 1890s. The dude ranch business then started to burgeon in the 1920s and the Dude Ranchers Association was founded in 1926. The dude ranch continues to thrive in such states as Arizona, Colorado, Idaho, Montana, Oregon, Texas and Wyoming.

DUNTON, WILLIAM HENRY

Henry Dunton (1874-1939) was an artist who painted pictures of cowboy life and other western scenes. Although born in Maine, he took various trips to the West where he sometimes worked as a ranch-hand as well as studying art and painting. His realistic depictions of cowboy life were popular in *Harper's* and *Scribner's* magazines. He became part of the Taos art community in 1912 and around 1920 he moved from New York to live in Taos.

E

EARP, MORGAN AND VIRGIL *see* EARP, WYATT.

EARP, WYATT

Wyatt Earp (1848-1929) was descended from a Virginian family who moved first to Illinois, where he was born, then to Kansas and then by wagon train to California. Earp worked as a teamster in California, Arizona and Wyoming, where he also refereed prizefights in the railroad camps. He took up buffalo-hunting in Kansas and at one time was in Ellsworth in Kansas.

Wichita

While there he was offered a job as marshal in 1873. This he refused but in 1874 he was offered and accepted the job of deputy marshal in Wichita. The offer came after Earp had been arrested for being involved in a fight and while under arrest had helped a deputy marshal to control a group of cowboys who were causing trouble in the town. It was quite common for cow towns such as Wichita to employ as part of the peacekeeping force hard men who had been on the other side of the law.

One of Earp's friends caused him a good deal of trouble when he became marshal. This was a Texas cattleman called Abel 'Shanghai' Pierce, who was noted for his drunkenness and fighting. Eventually Earp's services were no longer required in Wichita, perhaps for failing to hand over fines exacted from prostitutes or becoming involved in fights, and in 1876 he moved to Dodge City.

Dodge City

Dodge City, even by the standard of western towns of the time, had a reputation for violence and wildness. Indeed, it was known as the 'Gomorrah of the Plains'. Earp served on the town's peacekeeping force from 1876 until 1877 and from 1878 until 1879, becoming assistant marshal. While in Dodge City Earp succeeded in getting the better of Clay Allison. Allison, noted for his speed at drawing a gun, was beaten to the draw by Earp and instead of shooting Earp, Allison found himself leaving town. Also in Dodge City Earp had his life saved by John ('Doc') Holliday in 1878 when a band of cattle rustlers tried to gang up on him. Holliday shot one of the rustlers in the shoulder and helped to arrest the rest.

Tombstone

In 1879 Earp went to Tombstone, Arizona, at the invitation of his brother, Virgil, to the silver camp there, where Virgil was deputy marshal. Tombstone had attracted a great many people who were intent on getting rich quickly from the veins of silver found there. It was quite a wild place.

The Cowboys

Wyatt Earp became deputy sheriff at Pima County, and his brothers Jim, Morgan and Warren joined him there. The Earps and their wives became pillars of the community, and the business community looked to Wyatt and Virgil Earp to bring peace to the area. Particularly in need of controlling were members of a group known as 'the Cowboys', headed by N. H. ('Old Man') Clanton. They were given to drunken forays into town, and the business community, seeking to attract investment by mining capitalists and thus needing to convince them that the area was not so wild as it was supposed to be, was anxious to put an end to their antics.

In October 1880 the Cowboys and the peacekeeping force in Tombstone had a confrontation. Some of the Cowboys had ridden into town and started shooting it up. The marshal, Fred White, intervened and was shot dead, perhaps accidentally, by

Curly Bill Brocius. Wyatt Earp overcame him and put him in jail.

Old Man Clanton, having been killed when rustling in Mexico, was replaced as leader by his son, Ike. The situation between the Cowboys and the peacekeeping force hotted up.

In October 1881 Virgil Earp, now marshal of Tombstone, arrested Ike Clanton for carrying a weapon within the city limits, an act that was against the law. Fined for the offence, Clanton started shouting abuse at Morgan, brother of Virgil and Wyatt, who offered Ike a gun and suggested that they have a shoot-out. Clanton turned down the invitation. Meanwhile, another member of the Cowboy gang, Tom McLaury, had had a confrontation in the street with Wyatt.

OK Corral

The Earps decided that it was time to deal with the Cowboys once and for all. Virgil made Wyatt and Morgan deputy marshals. Doc Holliday, who had joined Wyatt in Tombstone, was also made a deputy marshal. Wyatt refused the offer of John Behan, sheriff of Cochise County, to disarm the Clantons and Tom McLaury and his brother, Frank, by peaceable means, perhaps because Behan was known to be a friend of the Cowboys.

Fremont Street next to the OK Corral was the scene of the confrontation between the Earps and the Cowboys. There is some disagreement as to who started the fight. John Behan blamed Wyatt Earp for taunting the Clantons and McLaurys, and the Earps claimed that Virgil asked the Cowboys to surrender but that they went for their guns instead. Another version has it that the fight was started by Doc Holliday who fired at Ike Clanton, narrowly missing him deliberately.

In any event, gunfire began and within thirty seconds Billy Clanton, brother of Ike, and Frank and Tom McLaury lay dead. The Earps and Holliday were still alive, although Virgil and

Morgan were wounded. There was controversy about the fight, known as the Battle of the OK Corral, and many people regarded the Earps and Holliday as murderers.

Pardon and retribution

The Earps and Holliday were tried for murder but were exonerated after a thirty-day court hearing on the grounds that the homicides were justified on the grounds of self-preservation. Virgil, however, was castigated for appointing his brothers and Holliday as deputy marshals and he was removed from his post of marshal.

Later the Earps were to pay a higher price for the confrontation of the OK Corral. Virgil received injuries in a night-time street ambush which invalided him for life, while Morgan was assassinated while he was playing pool, the major assassins being Frank Stilwell and Pete Spence, prominent members of the Cowboy gang, together with Florentino Cruz, an employee of Spence.

Revenge

Morgan's body was put on a train for their family home in California and it was accompanied by various members of the Earp family, Holliday and three friends of Wyatt who were noted gunmen. They were supposedly going to Morgan's funeral but the group left the train at Tucson and shot dead Stilwell and Cruz in revenge for Morgan's killing. Wyatt Earp was indicted for the murders and left Tombstone to work in the gold camps as a gambler, still with the indictment hanging over him.

Gambling

It was said of Wyatt as a card-player that he always had 'some dishonest trick', and he certainly appears to have made a lot of money from his gambling career and also from his silver-mining interests. In the 1890s he was able to retire from gambling and live on his ill-gotten gains.

Biography

Shortly before his death, Wyatt assisted Stuart Lake in writing his biography, *Wyatt Earp, Frontier Marshal*. Published in 1931, two years after Earp died, the book was more fabrication than fact. Lake later admitted that Earp had been so inarticulate that he had had to put words into his mouth in order to get the book written.

Film

John Ford's film *My Darling Clementine* (1946), starring Henry Fonda, although Western buffs regard it as a masterpiece, presents an overly sympathetic picture of Wyatt Earp and his association with Tombstone and it is low on fact, presumably because Earp, himself was responsible for giving Ford information. Thus both book and film present the myth rather than Wyatt Earp the real man, thanks partly to Earp himself.

EASTWOOD, CLINT

Clint Eastwood (1930–) is an American film actor who has acted in many films, several of them Westerns. He played Rowdy Yates in the CBS television western series *Rawhide*, set in Arizona. He also played a role in the spaghetti western *A Fistful of Dollars* (1964) and appeared in *A Few Dollars More* (1965) and in *The Good, the Bad and the Ugly* (1966).

Later he turned to directing and acted in several films which he directed, receiving an Oscar for best film and for best director for *Unforgiven* (1992). His western heroes are often more antiheroes or heroes with attitude, far away from the western heroes whom John Wayne portrayed.

EDGAR, HENRY

Henry Edgar was a goldminer who, with Bill Fairweather,

struck a major gold find at Alder Gulch in Montana in 1863. Miners had been encouraged to go to Montana to seek gold so that they could help finance the Civil War, some of the miners being on the side of the Confederates and some being on the side of the Union. Henry Edgar kept a journal that gives some indication of the excitement of making the find and of the importance of keeping it secret until it could be fully prospected and officially claimed. He also describes the dangers inherent in life as a prospector, particularly the dangers from the local Indian tribes who resented the intrusion of the goldminers into their lands.

EELS, MYRA

A missionary who, when newly married, crossed the Rockies in 1838 with her husband, Cushing, to take the gospel to the west. There were three other newly wed couples in their party, all being missionaries. They were William and Mary Gray, Asa and Sarah Smith and Elkanah and Mary Walker. The news of the successful journey was greeted with enthusiasm in the east and it was the signal for tens of thousands of women between 1840 and 1869 (when the transcontinental railroad was completed) to join the trek westwards.

All three women kept journals. They wrote of the lack of privacy and their annoyance at each other's habits and behaviour, an annoyance exacerbated by the proximity of each other. They also wrote of the hardships of the journey—the long hours spent on horseback, the storms and floods, the extreme cold, the gnat bites, the lack of food and the unpleasantness of it when they had it (buffalo tongues being a sample menu), the lack of food for the horses and the agony of having to keep travelling and working, however ill they felt. If the women in the east who were to follow after them had read the journals they would certainly not have been so eager to migrate to the west.

ELLSWORTH, KANSAS

Ellsworth was one of several towns in Kansas that became both famous and infamous as cow towns during the 1870s. As the name indicates, the cattle industry was of major importance in these towns. There was often a lot of money around the cow towns. Cattle were bought and sold and money changed hands while the said towns, being the end of the cattle trails, also saw the payment of the cowboys who had spent months on the trail.

Money made in these ways was cause for celebration, celebration that often ended in wildness and trouble. Gambling and prostitution also went hand in hand with money and were also causes of trouble. The mixture of people common in the cow towns did not help matters, as there were stockmen selling and buying cattle, cowboys enjoying leisure after long months of hard work and perhaps looking for work when their money ran out, land speculators out to make as much money as possible, buffalo hunters, soldiers from the frontier posts, saloon-keepers and prostitutes. This mixture was often a recipe for disaster.

To demonstrate the level of violence that could beset the cow towns, Ellsworth had eight homicides in its first year as a cow town. The violence was added to by the presence of the English-born Thompson brothers, Ben and Bill, who had served in the Confederate army. In Ellsworth they ran a saloon and gambling hall and were generally noted for their drunkenness and lawlessness. The situation was not helped by the fact that one of the men appointed in Ellsworth to keep law and order was himself a gunfighter and hard man who had lived on the wrong side of the law in California. He was John Morco, known as 'Happy Jack' Morco, and he antagonized the Thompson brothers among others of the inhabitants of Ellsworth. It was, in fact, quite common for men with a history as lawless gunfighters to be appointed to the peacekeeping force in a western town as it was supposed that they would be better at keeping order.

Ellsworth began operating as a cattle town in 1871, and the Kansas Pacific Railroad gave a good deal of financial support to the development of the town and to the development of a new cattle trail, called, not surprisingly, the Ellsworth Cattle Trail. Ellsworth seemed set to be a boom town but in the late summer of 1873 the cattle market in Kansas collapsed suddenly because of financial panic and many people involved in the cattle trade in Ellsworth were made bankrupt. The temporary collapse of the cattle trade not only proved the end of many people involved in it but it also meant the end of Ellsworth as a major cow town. Its end was hastened by the opening of a branch of the Santa Fe Railway to Wichita, which more or less took over Ellsworth role. *See* ABILENE; THOMPSON BROTHERS; and WICHITA.

EVANS, DALE

Dale Evans (1912–) was the second wife of Roy Rogers who appeared and sang in many Westerns. Dale Evans featured in many films with her husband, the first being *The Cowboy and the Senorita* (1944) and appeared with him on a long-running TV series. Evans and Rogers were regarded as good role models for family life as violence, particularly violence involving gunfire, was kept to a minimum in the films in which they appeared. *See* ROGERS, ROY.

EXODUSTERS

The Exodusters was the name adopted by the African Americans who left their homes in the south and began moving west. The name was based on the biblical Exodus, the name given to the migration of the Hebrews from Egypt to the Promised Land.

Some of the Exodusters travelled west by riverboat up the Mississippi and the Missouri Rivers and some went by train. Many of them were, however, very poor and could not afford these forms of transport and had no choice but to walk to the land that they hoped would provide them with a more comfortable, more affluent life. It was a very long walk from such states as Louisiana, Kentucky and Tennessee to Kansas, a distance of more than five hundred miles.

Although slavery was made illegal after the Civil War, conditions for black people in the south were still very bad and they were very poor. They had their freedom, but the white people still had the land and it was too expensive for former slaves to buy. Thus they were forced either to rent land from the white landowners or to become involved in sharecropping.

Benjamin 'Pap' Singleton

In 1873 Benjamin Singleton, known as 'Pap', having heard of the 'homestead scheme' by which the government was offering homesteads of 160 acres in the west to anyone who paid a fee of ten dollars and was prepared to work the land for five years, went to Kansas to see for himself. He returned to his home in Tennessee and set about persuading African Americans to take advantage of the opportunities to be had in the west. This he did by printing and distributing leaflets advertising these advantages.

A few hundred African Americans moved to a place in Kansas which became known as the Singleton Colony and others moved to other parts of Kansas. News of the opportunities available in the west got back to the south via letters written by the settlers to family and friends still at home.

Rumour

It was not the pleas of Singleton, nor the news sent from Kansas back home, which had the biggest influence on the decision of many African Americans to travel the hundreds of miles west— it was the effect of rumour. In 1879 a rumour began circulating to the effect that the whole of Kansas had been set aside by the government for the use of former slaves and that every black family who could get to Kansas would be supplied with free land and 500 dollars. This rumour had in fact no basis in truth but it inspired many thousands of African Americas to travel to Kansas, however arduous the journey.

Of course when they got there they discovered the fallacy of the rumour but most of them decided to stay all the same, given the conditions back home and the prospect of a long return journey. Some of them stayed in the towns of Kansas but most of them settled on farms or in small communities. The largest settlement of Exodusters was in Nocodemus in western Kansas.

The fortunes of the African Americans were as varied as those of other settlers. Some prospered, some simply stuck it out, some moved farther west, and some gave up and went home. Singleton died poor in 1892 in Topeka, Kansas, at the age of eighty-three but he had helped at least some of the Exodusters on the path to a better life.

F

FAUST, FREDERICK SCHILLER
Frederick Faust (1892-1944) was a prolific writer of pulp fiction in several genres, including Westerns. He wrote under many pseudonyms and his most popular books appeared under the name Max Brand. He is regarded as contributing greatly to the creation of the western romantic myth.

FIELDS, MARY
Mary Fields was an example, although admittedly an unusual one, of the new breed of women that was born as a result of the opening up of the west. Born a slave in Tennessee, she moved to

Cascade in Montana when she was over fifty years of age and set about proving that a woman could do most things that a man could do. A tall, heavy woman, she hauled freight for St Peter's Catholic Mission twenty miles outside Cascade, usually armed with both a revolver and a rifle to ward off attack, whether this was from wolves or people.

Having been sacked by the mission for her bizarre ways, she opened a restaurant in Cascade which failed to do well because of her habit of giving free meals to the needy. There are many stories of her independence, competence and big-heartedness.

When she was in her sixties she was given a job driving the mail, only the second woman in America to do so. Her ability to get the mail to its destination as quickly as possible and her determination to deliver it, no matter what the weather conditions were, made her a legend in the area. In her seventies, when she was too old to keep on driving the mail van, she opened a laundry in her home.

Everyone admired her spirit and capacity for hard work, and her capacity to drink was recognized by the fact that she was the first woman to be officially granted the privilege of being allowed to drink in the saloons of Cascade, something that women were usually forbidden to do. The men of Cascade were wont to admit that she could drink more whiskey than they could. She died in 1914.

FONDA, HENRY

Henry Fonda (1905-82) was an American stage and film actor who was born in Nebraska. He had a long and distinguished career, being particularly noted for his performances in such films as *The Young Mr Lincoln* (1939), *The Grapes of Wrath* (1940), *Twelve Angry Men* (1957) and *On Golden Pond* (1981), for which he received an Academy Award.

He appeared in several westerns. In *My Darling Clementine*

(1946), directed by John Ford and held to be one of the great classics by many Western buffs, Fonda played the part of Wyatt Earp. Other Westerns in which he appeared include *The Tin Star* (1957) and *Warlock* (1959).

FOOTE, MARY

Mary Foote is known as a writer of novels that portray life in the rough silver mining towns of California. Mary Halock, as she was before her marriage, was a successful illustrator in New York when she married in 1876 a young civil engineer called Arthur Foote. Foote was not content to remain in New York but wished to try his hand at making his fortune in the West. They thus gave up their comfortable lives in the east and went west, to New Almaden in California, to be exact.

Mary Foote, not surprisingly, was rather homesick and kept up her home ties by having a regular correspondence with Richard Gilder and his wife, Helena, Gilder being the editor of *Scribner's Monthly*. Gilder was so impressed by the vivid accounts of his correspondent's new environment and the conditions and inhabitants there that he put some of them together and published them as articles in his magazine. Mary Foote then began writing articles herself and moved on to fiction by writing short stories, often illustrating her work.

When she and her husband moved to Leadville, Colorado, a western boom town at that time, Mary turned to novel-writing, her best-known novel being *The Lead Horse Claim*, a romance set against the background of the boom in silver mining in Leadville. Although she based her novels on her environment and on the people around her, she made no mention of the brutality, violence or squalor that surrounded her but from which she was protected by her gender and her status.

There was one area of life in Leadville about which she could write with experience. This was the situation of the women who had been relocated from comfortable lives in the east to much more basic frontier lives in the West. In her novel *The Last Assembly Ball*, she wrote of the wrench that women felt when they had to be apart from family, friends, culture, lifestyle and all that they had known.

FORD, BOB

Bob Ford has gone down in history as the man who shot the infamous outlaw Jesse James, although he was a member of the James gang. Governor Crittenden of Missouri, tired of the robbery and killing perpetrated by James and his men, persuaded the railroads, which had suffered several times from train hold-ups carried out by James, to contribute towards a reward of $10,000 to be given to anyone who would bring in Jesse James, and his brother Frank, dead or alive.

The facts of how the killing came to take place are not at all clear. Some sources indicate that Bob Ford, with his brother Charlie, saw the notice advertising the reward and could not resist it. Others indicate that Governor Crittenden approached Ford and asked him to do it. In any event, the killing was carried out by Ford and its manner has become a legend.

On the morning of 3 April 1882, Bob Ford went to the house in St Joseph, Missouri, where Jesse James, under his alias of J.D. Howard, was living with his wife and children. Ford is said to have told Crittenden later that, when he arrived at James's house, James was standing on a chair dusting or straightening a picture on the wall and so having his back to Ford as he walked in. Before James could turn around, Ford shot him just behind the ear and he fell down dead. For this act of shooting a man with his back to him, Ford is remembered in song as 'the dirty little coward who shot Mr Howard', although it has to be borne in mind that Jesse James himself was no angel.

As a pure technicality, Ford was tried for murder and was sentenced to death. He was immediately pardoned by Crittenden but was murdered ten years later by a man called Kelley.

FORD, JOHN
John Ford (1895-1973), born Sean Aloysius O'Feeny, was an American film director who made a great contribution to the development of the western film. He directed his first western film in 1917 and two more in the 1920s, but Ford was also interested in other film genres and concentrated on these for a while before returning to the Western in 1939 with *Stagecoach*, a film that established Ford as the foremost director of Westerns and also made a star of John Wayne, who was to have a long and distinguished career in western films.

Ford has been particularly praised for the way in which he was able to make landscape an essential and vivid part of his films. His early Westerns celebrated the glorious victory of supposed eastern civilization over supposed western barbarism, and in several cases his films have been criticized for demonstrating racist feelings against the native North American Indians, such as the Comanches.

He worked with the western filmstars of the day—John Wayne, Henry Fonda, James Stewart and Ward Bond—and his early films include *My Darling Clementine* (1946), a film about Wyatt Earp starring Henry Fonda, and the cavalry trilogy starring John Wayne, *Fort Apache* (1948), *She wore a Yellow Ribbon* (1949) and *Rio Grande* (1950). His later films, post-1950, present a more complex view of the West.

FORTY-NINERS
Forty-niners was the name given to the people who took part in the goldrush of 1849. Gold had been discovered in California and there was a massive migration there with a view to getting rich quick. *See* GOLDRUSH.

FREMONT, JOHN CHARLES

Lieutenant John Charles Fremont was sent by the American government to travel in the West and make better maps of the area. He was accompanied by scout and guide Kit Carson, and they made three major expeditions in the 1840s.

They explored the Great Salt Lake in Utah, sailing on a rubber boat. They also explored the very hot deserts of Nevada and came close to starvation when climbing over the mountains of the Sierra Nevada during the winter. Fremont and Carson took part in the war with Mexico that made California a part of the United States of America. The names of Fremont and Carson were given to various places that they explored and mapped.

When Fremont was exploring parts of Nevada around Pyramid Lake he met the chief of the Paiutes, Winnemucca, and became friendly with him. The chief agreed to accompany the party across the mountains to California.

The trip that Fremont and Carson took through Nevada, across the Sierra and into California was to lead to a marked increase in the settlement of Oregon. Fremont's report on the region was so enthusiastic, lengthy and detailed that the government ordered 100,000 copies of it. People rushed to read about the wonders of the area as described by the flamboyant Fremont, sometimes known as 'Pathfinder'. Between 1845 and 1847 several thousand people set out on the trail to Oregon. With the trail now marked in detail they felt much more optimistic about making the lengthy overland journey. *See* CARSON, KIT.

FUR TRADE

Fur played a part in the opening up of the West. The French and the British had early on identified the importance of North America as a source of fur, particularly beaver. The British formed the Hudson's Bay Company in the late 1660s and after the British victory over the French in 1763 Britain acquired a virtual monopoly in the fur trade in North America.

However, after the American War of Independence, Americans decided that it was time to take advantage of the profits that could be made from the fur trade. As the trade boomed, the supply of beaver diminished and the fur traders had to make their way farther and farther into the interior to trap.

Some of the traders worked for one of the several fur companies, such as the American Fur Company started by John Jacob Astor in 1808, which sprang up over the country, and some worked for themselves as free trappers and traders. Theoretically the free trappers, sometimes called mountain men, got the best of the deal because they could make more money, but their financial situation was often hazardous and payment for fur was slow. The company men's potential earnings were small but at least they were regular. Whether attached to a company or not, the men's work was hazardous because of the climate and the danger from grizzly bears or Indians, and it was lonely.

A great many of the trappers, especially the African American trappers, took Indian women as wives. In many cases they paid for them. The women were not only a source of company but they could help with the work of trapping and might ensure friendly relations with the Indian tribes.

The Indians played an important part in the fur trade in North America, especially in the case of fur traders and trappers who were company men. As well as trapping for pelts they bought from the Indians. The white fur traders acquired their pelts, usually beaver pelts, by trapping but the Indians preferred not to use traps, acquiring their pelts by hunting. The Indians did not come out profitably from the barter of furs, as some of the things they were given in exchange included blankets, beads, mirrors, tobacco, salt, guns, ammunition, knives, rum and whisky. The whisky and rum were to speed their downfall.

The beaver trade was particularly lucrative as there was much demand in Europe for beaver fur. Not only was the fur a favourite with affluent women for coats and muffs, but the beaver's underfur was much used in the hat trade to make men's hats. Not long after Astor sold his shares in the American Fur Company (1834) and retired, the beaver trade began to decline, this being due in great part to the use of silk instead of beaver in the hat trade. By 1840 the beaver fur trade was largely at an end. *See* ASTOR, JOHN JACOB and ROCKY MOUNTAIN FUR COMPANY.

G

GARRETT, PAT
Pat Garrett has gone down in history as the killer of the outlaw Billy the Kid. He was originally a Texan buffalo hunter and he was made sheriff of Lincoln, Wyoming, with a view to putting an end to Billy the Kid, since everyone was tired of his lawless and murderous behaviour. Garrett had known Billy in Texas and is said to have once been a card-playing friend of his.

Surrender of Billy the Kid
Garrett put together a posse of deputies and set out to track down Billy. They cornered him and some of his men in an abandoned house near Stinking Springs in December 1880. Eventually Billy surrendered and was sent for trial for some of the killings that he had committed. He was found guilty and sentenced to death.

Escape of Billy the Kid
Billy was locked in a room above Murphy's old general store in Lincoln and was kept under heavy guard in handcuffs and leg irons. There are various versions of how Billy succeeded in es-

caping in April 1881. The most common version is that on the day that Garrett was out of town arranging for his hanging, Billy asked one of the deputies, J. W. Bell, to take him to the toilet and then slipped the handcuffs off his thin wrists. Again there are variations on the story of how he got the gun. One version suggests that he grabbed the deputy's gun while another has it that a friend hid a gun in the toilet while visiting him.

By whatever means he got the gun, Billy used it to shoot Bell. He is then said to have grabbed a shotgun from Garrett's office and shot Bob Ollinger, the other guard. Having shot Ollinger, Billy managed to release himself from his leg shackles, stole a horse, said goodbye to some of the inhabitants and rode out of town. A reward was offered for the capture of the outlaw, and Garrett set out to bring him in.

Death of Billy the Kid

Some weeks were to pass before Garrett found out where his quarry was. He was in Fort Sumner visiting his girlfriend, Paulita Maxwell, the likelihood being that he was told of Billy's presence by Pete Maxwell, brother of Paulita, who disapproved of his sister's relationship with the outlaw. On the evening of 14 July 1881, Garrett and his posse reached the Maxwell house.

Billy was in the porch with a meat knife in his hand, being about to cut some meat from a steer hanging there, and on hearing or seeing someone on the porch ducked into one of the bedrooms where Garrett was waiting for him. Garrett fired twice at Billy and the first shot killed him. Opinions vary as to whether or not Billy was armed.

Garrett was not slow to capitalize on his association with such a well-known outlaw. He had his somewhat exaggerated account of Billy the Kid's life ghostwritten by an itinerant newspaperman, Ash Upson, and published under the title of *The Authentic Life of Billy the Kid*.

Pat Garrett then held various jobs and acquired a ranch in New Mexico. When it failed, he began to drink too much and he embarked on a feud with a neighbour. He was killed by the neighbour in 1908. *See* BILLY THE KID.

GERONIMO

Geronimo was a warrior leader of the Apaches. He was the leader of a band of Apaches known as the Bedonkohe Apache who had become assimilated into the Chiricahua. He was born Goyahkla but was given the name Geronimo by the Mexicans because they prayed to St Geronimo for salvation when he was fighting against them with great ferocity for having murdered his family. On the death of Cochise, chief of the Chiricahua Apache, his son, Taza, became chief, but, because Taza lacked authority and leadership many of the Chiricahua Apaches looked to Geronimo for leadership.

General Crook had subdued the Apaches and settled them in reservations in 1873. Geronimo could not bear the monotony of reservation life, and he and some of his men went off to make raids in Mexico. He was particularly determined to stay out of reservations after the 1875 consolidation of the reservations by which the Apaches were all to be accommodated into one over-crowded reservation at San Carlos.

John Clum

However, he made a mistake which cost him his liberty for a time. He had been in Mexico but decided to visit the reservation at Warm Springs early in 1877. The discipline there was very lax and several border raiders stayed there occasionally. Word of Geronimo's presence was wired to the agent in charge of the San Carlos reservation, John Clum, and he was ordered to arrest Geronimo. He did so by a trick.

Clum set out for Warm Springs with 100 of his Apache police. On arrival he sent word to Geronimo and other chiefs who had left the reservation that he wished to speak to them. Not scenting trouble, they agreed to this. They found Clum sitting with just a few policemen and, when Clum accused Geronimo of killing people and violating the agreement which had been struck between Cochise and the American government and told him that he was taking him to San Carlos, Geronimo defied him. He refused to go to San Carlos and threatened to kill Clum and his Apache policemen.

Then Clum touched the brim of his hat, which was a prearranged signal for the rest of his policemen to appear. Geronimo did not resist and was taken to San Carlos in chains. It was the only time that Geronimo was captured.

Conditions at San Carlos were even worse than he expected but he was incarcerated and the reservation was under guard by the cavalry. He had no choice but to stay put for a time but he escaped to Mexico with some of his men after about a year, voluntarily returning in 1880 after a bitterly cold winter in the mountains when he and his men nearly starved to death.

Escape
In September 1881 a religious movement preached the rising again of the Apache way of life and the demise of the white man. This alarmed the authorities and they sent troops to arrest the leader of the movement, Noch-ay-del-klinne. A pitched battle followed and some Apaches and some troops were killed. Geronimo is said not to have been party to this movement but a rumour went around that he was to be hanged and the other Apache chiefs arrested. He and a band of warriors immediately left the reservation to return six months later in April 1882 to persuade most of the Chiricahuas to leave with him for Mexico.

Guerrilla warfare
They were pursued by the cavalry but the Apache men succeeded in fighting a rearguard action with the women and chil-

dren at the front. Unfortunately a Mexican infantry regiment set upon the front of the regiment and killed many of the women and children. Geronimo and some others escaped and joined with some other Indians to form a guerrilla band to get their revenge on the Mexicans. For the next two years they raided Mexican towns and villages, sometimes also attacking American settlements and ranches.

Peace

By this time the authorities were tired of the action of Geronimo and his band of warriors. They also thought that it was time to do something about the grievances of the Apaches who had remained on the San Carlos reservation. In order to investigate the nature of these grievances and do something about them and in order to stop Geronimo. For the rest of the Geronimo story, *see* Geronimo under APACHES.

GHOST DANCE

The ghost dance was a ritual dance that became popular among some Indian tribes in 1889. They believed that, if they took part in this dance, their old way of life would come back—the buffalo would return and with them would return the Indians' freedom to roam the range freely. By this time the Indians were leading rather sad lives. They were confined to reservations and their chiefs were deprived of their former power and glory. The government, having got the Indians where they wanted them, were not very generous when it came to food and clothes and, to make matters worse, the West suffered a major drought in 1889 that brought hunger and disease to the reservations. It was a time to dream about the past and to fantasize about the future.

Wovoka

The ghost dance was brought to the Indians in 1889 by Wovoka of the Paiutes who were located in Nevada. He was the son of

Tavibo, a minor chief, who claimed to have had a revelation made to him in 1870. This revelation indicated that all the people on earth would be destroyed and that at the end of three days the Indians would be resurrected and would enjoy their old way of life again. People were sceptical of this but, as the years went on, Tavibo claimed to have further revelations, in one of which it was revealed to him that in order to get their old life back the Indians had to dance and to go on dancing.

Tavibo died, and his son was adopted by a white family named Wilson and became known as Jack Wilson. Jack Wilson or Wovoka, however, did not forget his father and his revelations, and in time he himself began to claim to have revelations. He claimed to have been taken to the world of the Great Spirit and to have been given details of a dance to give to his people. This was the ghost dance.

The ghost dance involved the Indians forming a large circle and dancing and chanting as they alternately widened and constricted the circle. The dance went on for several days.

Sioux

The dance caught the imagination of many of the other tribes and within a few weeks the Indian tribes of the Rocky Mountains were all engaged in performing the ghost dance. News of the dance soon spread to other tribes across the country, including the Indians of the plains, such as the Cheyenne and the Sioux. The Sioux, in particular, took up the performing of the ghost dance with great fervour. They added a few refinements of their own in that they danced round a sacred tree and wore shirts, 'ghost shirts', painted with magical symbols, supposedly designed to keep away the white men's bullets. They danced so much, and often so fast, that they often reached a state of frenzy or ecstasy. Their accompanying chants often referred to the coming of the buffalo.

Sitting Bull

Sitting Bull, formerly a great war-leader of the Sioux and chief of the Huncpapa Sioux, but at this point in retirement at the Standing Rock reservation, expressed an interest in having his tribe taught the ghost dance and the authorities grew alarmed. They had a healthy respect for Sitting Bull and they were afraid that the Indians were once again to be a cause of trouble. It was suggested that troops be sent to the Sioux reservations but caution was urged in case the troops panicked the Indians.

The agent in charge of Standing Rock decided that the best thing to do was to take Sitting Bull into custody himself and gave orders to his Sioux police to go to Siting Bull's cabin and bring him in. Lieutenant Bull Head was in charge and asked the chief to go with him. Sitting Bull at first agreed but got annoyed when the police began to search his cabin for weapons.

The police started manhandling the chief and a riot broke out between the Sioux police and the Sioux followers of Sitting Bull when the chief said that he was not going to go with the police. In the fracas one of the chief's followers, Catch the Bear, fired at Lieutenant Bull Head and wounded him in the side. As he fell he fired at his assailant but hit Sitting Bull in the chest. Meanwhile one of the Sioux policemen, Red Tomahawk, shot Sitting Bull through the head. On the death of the chief a free-for-all ensued and only the arrival of the cavalry saved all the policemen from being killed.

The death of Sitting Bull led to the tragedy of Wounded Knee. *See* WOUNDED KNEE.

GOLDRUSH

There were several reasons for the opening up of the west but a major one of these was gold. On 24 January 1848 James W. Marshall, when inspecting a sawmill on the ranch of John Sutter on the Sierra Nevada, found traces of gold in a millrace. He told

Sutter and tests were undertaken to establish whether or not gold was present. The tests proved positive. Sutter suggested keeping the matter a secret but this was a vain hope, since so many workmen had heard about the find, and the news spread like wildfire, especially to the town of San Francisco.

Gold fever in California

Much of the news was spread there by a local merchant named Sam Brannan, who saw an opportunity to make a great deal of money by selling tools and supplies to those looking for gold. It was thus in his interest to help to create as major a gold rush as possible.

Gold fever gripped San Francisco and spread rapidly. In December 1848 President James Polk confirmed the rumours of gold, which had spread to Washington by then. A sample of Californian gold dust was put on display by way of even greater confirmation. America went gold mad and other parts of the world joined in. Grossly exaggerated rumours spread about the amount of gold available and the ease with which it could be found and extracted. By this time it was 1849 and the day of the 'forty-niner' had arrived, 'forty-niner' being the term given to anyone affected by the gold fever.

There were several routes to California and its gold. For many the most convenient way was by sailing ship round Cape Horn. The disadvantages of this method of approaching the supposed goldfields were that it took a very long time—as much as six months—and that it was very expensive. A shorter way by sea was via the Panamanian isthmus but this was still expensive and dangerous.

Many people opted to undertake the journey to California overland, the two main routes being the Oregon Trail and the Santa Fe or Mormon Trail. The forty-niners suffered all the hardships of earlier pioneers and more, for many of them were so eager to get rich quick that they failed to equip themselves adequately and, in addition, many were so used to town life that they found life on the trail even more difficult than those who had more realistic expectations. To make matters worse, the spring of 1849 was particularly wet and wagons floundered in the mud and a cholera epidemic claimed many lives.

The population of California leapt to unbelievable proportions. At first the gold was relatively easy to extract, given some hard work, because the gold was relatively superficial and could be obtained by digging and then putting the soil and what was thought to be gold in a pan and swilling water around it until the gold was revealed. As the gold became harder to find, people were quick to move on as rumours of new strikes spread. Many were sure that a fortune was just round the corner.

Very few people attained great wealth in the Californian gold rush. Many of those who did make any money spent it almost immediately. People involved in selling supplies and providing accommodation capitalized on the situation by charging huge amounts. There was much entertainment for the successful prospector, particularly drinking, gambling which often led to fighting. Prostitution was rife and there was a high level of lawlessness and much racism, particularly against the Chinese.

By the mid 1850s, as far as the average prospector was concerned, the Californian gold rush was coming to an end. The region had been thoroughly prospected and the gold that was relatively near the surface had been removed. Deeper finds had to be left to operators with the appropriate expensive equipment to get at the gold. By this time gold prospecting for many had become a way of life and they looked for other potential sites to prospect.

Gold in Colorado

There were reports of various strikes but real hope came to the prospectors with the news that gold had been discovered in Colorado. In 1859 William Green Russell struck gold in the area near Pike's Peak and another gold rush was born, the number of people rushing to Colorado being augmented by people who had lost money in the Panic of 1857 and who wished to get their hands on some money quickly. This time fewer people were content with the surface gold and shafts were sunk to get at the richer veins of gold. Men not only prospected themselves but were employed in the mines that proliferated. Not only gold was mined but also silver, and some people acquired great wealth in the area.

Gold in Nevada and Montana

Other areas also had successful strikes. Nevada, particularly the Washoe field, also became a focus for gold prospectors, and in the summer of 1859 the lucrative Ophir Vein was discovered at Six Mile Canyon by Peter O'Riley and Patrick McLaughlin, although they took into partnership three men who said that they owned the claim, chief among these being Henry Comstock.

Gold fever then moved north to Idaho and then proceeded to Montana. It was in Montana that the major gold discovery was made by Henry Edgar and Bill Fairweather, which they named Alder Gulch. A good picture of the life of the goldminer was given by Edgar in the journal that he kept.

Gold in Dakota

Life for the gold prospectors and miners was never easy. The work was hard and it could be dangerous in that there were many accidents involving falling down mine-shafts or mine cave-ins but the rush to the gold discovery in 1874 at the Black Hills of Dakota was particularly dangerous because that was an area inhabited by the Sioux. Even the Sioux with their fierce reputation, however, could not stop people from rushing to try to get rich.

The end of the American gold rush

There was another major gold strike at Cripple Creek in Colorado in 1890 but after that the focus of gold-mining moved north to Alaska and the Klondike River in Canada. However, gold had left a great legacy in America. Not only did some people become rich but it had really opened up the country and brought people to areas to which they would never otherwise have gone. After a goldrush was over and people moved on to the next strike, there were usually some who stayed on. In addition, gold brought a demand for transport and communication and the stagecoach, the railway, the telegraph and the Pony Express owe their development across the continent to gold.

GOODNIGHT, CHARLES

Charles Goodnight (1836-1929) was a cattleman who invented the first chuckwagon. By 1857 he was running a herd on the Palo Pinto range in Texas. During the Civil War he worked as a scout for a Confederate frontier regiment and after the war he teamed up with Oliver Loving to raise and sell cattle.

Chuckwagon

Many Texans were looking to the north to sell their cattle but Goodnight and Loving decided to look to the west and made for Fort Sumner in New Mexico. It was on this journey that he devised the 'chuckwagon', which was to prove so popular with travellers in the west. He bought the base of an old army wagon and had it rebuilt with the very tough wood that the Indians used for their bows and replaced the original wooden axles with iron axles, using a can of tallow for lubrication purposes. Instead of having the wagon pulled by horses he had it pulled by a team of oxen. At the rear of the wagon he had constructed a large box with compartments and with a hinged lid that could be dropped down to make a worktop for cooks. Copies of this chuckwagon were soon to be seen all over the trails of the west.

Trailblazing

When Goodnight and Loving got to Fort Sumner after an arduous journey, they failed to sell the herd of cattle as such to the government contractor but, because there were several thousand Navahos there requiring to be fed by the government, they were able to sell many of the steers on the hoof as beef at a very good price. Loving moved on to Colorado with the unsold cows and calves and sold them to John Iliff there while Goodnight returned to Texas for more cattle, after which he, too, made his way to Colorado. The routes trailblazed by Goodnight and Loving to New Mexico and Colorado became standard cattle trails and became known as the Horsehead Route and the Goodnight-Loving Trail.

Death of Loving

The partnership of Goodnight and Loving ended with the tragic death of Loving following the amputation of his arm, which had become gangrenous after sustaining a severe wound in a confrontation with the Comanches. It was ironic that Loving should die in that way because he had had a miraculous escape from the Comanches, holding out against them single-handed and then making his way towards Fort Sumner.

Goodnight continued to drive cattle to Colorado but in 1868 he sold his herd to John Iliff and ranged cattle on the Bosque Grande in New Mexico, later taken over by John Chisum, who was later to be part of the story of Billy the Kid. For a while he prospered as a rancher in Colorado, having got married to Mary Ann Dyer, but, in common with many others, he was financially very badly affected by the Panic of 1873.

Panhandle

Having tried and failed for two years to make a recovery, he decided to make for Texas and set out in the autumn of 1875 with a herd of two thousand cattle. In the spring of 1876 he moved into the Panhandle and selected the Palo Duro as being the perfect location for his ranch. There was a copious water supply, excellent grassland and no need for fencing. Goodnight originally named his ranch Old Home Ranch.

JA Ranch
In a chance meeting in Colorado, Goodnight met a wealthy Irishman named John Adair who offered to finance a major cattle venture in a million-acre ranch in the Palo Duro to be named JA Ranch after Adair. The JA Ranch was hugely profitable, especially after the introduction of Herefords which proved suited to the area.

Cattaloes
After eleven years Goodnight decided to withdraw from the JA Ranch and start again on his own about 60 miles from his original Old Home Ranch. He conducted experiments on crossbreeding buffalo and cattle and produced cattaloes which proved not to be successful as meat-producers.

Sidesaddles
Although Goodnight is mainly remembered as the inventor of the chuckwagon, he also turned his powers of invention to saddles, in particular saddles designed specifically for women. At that time women rode sidesaddle, it being considered unsuitable for them to straddle horses. The sidesaddle used was not really suitable for some of the lively horses that were common on the range, and there were a number of accidents. Goodnight designed a safer sidesaddle and persuaded his usual saddle-maker to make up a few as an experiment. The saddle was an immediate success and such sidesaddles became generally popular in the West.

Charles Goodnight died in 1929 at the age of ninety-three.

GREAT BLIZZARD

The Great Blizzard took place during the winter of 1886-87, which was to be the worst in the history of the West. In fact, it consisted of several blizzards, the first of which occurred in November and brought much deeper snow than usual to the northern plains. Another occurred three weeks later and brought stagecoach travel in Wyoming to a complete halt. A third blizzard occurred in early January of 1887, bringing snow at the rate of one inch an hour and temperatures that plummeted to 46 degrees Fahrenheit below zero. Worse was yet to come on 28 January. Yet another blizzard occurred and brought devastation to the cattle herds. Thousands of them died, frozen or starved to death or suffocated in drifts. Some staggered into the towns desperately in search of food and warmth. They uprooted newly planted trees.

The animals were not the only casualties. Many cowboys froze to death trying to help the cattle, and families died of hypothermia. The extent of the devastation was not fully known until spring came and it was discovered that some ranchers had lost as much as 90 per cent of their herds. Some ranchers and cowboys were so affected by the suffering of the animals that they vowed never to be involved with the cattle industry again.

Many people were left with crippling debts and off-loaded any remaining cattle onto the market in order to meet these. The price of cattle fell dramatically and many ranchers went bankrupt. Those who remained in the cattle industry were to find that it was never the same after the Great Blizzard.

The industry changed completely. Ranchers put up fences to confine their cattle rather than let them roam freely on the ranges. Crops were grown for winter feed for the cattle so that they were not again left to forage for themselves in a hard winter. The role of the cowboy also changed significantly. Less time was spent on the range, apart from rounding up the cattle or calves, and more on duties around the ranch. Undoubtedly the Great Blizzard had far-reaching effects on life in the west.

GREY, ZANE

Zane Grey (1872-1939) was a prolific writer of western novels. Born Pearl Zane Gray in Ohio, he read the cheap novels popular in the 1890s when he was a young man and got a taste both for Westerns and for writing. Since his father was opposed to writing as a career, he became a dentist but he did not give up his writing dreams and eventually gave up dentistry to devote himself to writing.

A trip to the west with his new bride in 1906 stirred an interest in writing about it, and in 1907 a trip to Arizona furthered this interest when he heard tales about outlaws, cowboys, Indians, etc. He had the first of his romanticized western novels, *The Heritage of the Desert*, published in 1909 and followed this with other desert novels.

From 1907 he spent about ten years travelling in the southwest and in Mexico and Cuba gathering material for his books. His published works include fifty-six books with western settings, and his presentation of a romanticized mythical West coloured many people's perception of life in the Old West. His novels include *Riders of the Purple Sage* (1912), *Wild Fire* (1917), *Fighting Caravans* (1928, *The Lost Wagon Train* (1936) and *Knights of the Range* (1939).

GUERIN, ELIZABETH (*or* ELSA) JANE FOREST

Elizabeth (or Elsa) Guerin spent around thirteen years of her life disguised as a man, several of these in the West. The illegitimate daughter of a Louisiana planter, she ran off at the age of twelve to St Louis with a man named Forest who was a pilot on a Mississippi riverboat.

When she was sixteen and had borne two children her husband was killed by one of his crew, called Jamieson, and she was left with no means of support. She felt that the only thing she could do was to leave her children in the care of the Sisters of Charity and disguise herself as a man to find work, there being few work opportunities for women. She obtained work as a cabin boy on a steamer which went between St Louis and New Orleans and she worked on the steamer for four years, once a month changing back into women's clothes to visit her children.

Having lost her job on the steamer, she obtained work as a brakeman on the Illinois Central Railroad. However, after a few months she realized that the conductor had seen through her disguise and she fled.

Her disguise was discovered when she was wounded in a shoot-out with Jamieson, the killer of her husband. The woman who found her injured was sympathetic to her plight and gave her refuge and kept her secret.

In 1855, excited by the prospect of gold in California, she set out on a 60-man expedition there but when she got there the weather was bad, prices were very high and she was not physically strong enough for prospecting. Instead she got a job as a cleaner in a saloon and six months later bought a partnership in a saloon with her savings. Eight months later she sold her share in the saloon at a profit and began trading in mules, then going into freighting by shipping and transporting goods by mule train to the gold camps in the mountains.

Having returned to St Louis to see her children, she went back to California overland, taking mules, horses and cattle. Although the journey was arduous and many of the cattle died she had enough left to open a small ranch. Soon she sold her ranch and mule-freight business, and, having made quite a lot of money, went back home to St Louis as a woman.

She soon tired of her inactive life as a woman and first joined the American Fur Company as a trader but then opened a saloon in Denver, known as 'Mountain Boy's Saloon', she herself becoming known as 'Mountain Charley'. Her identity as a woman was revealed by Jamieson, whom she met accidentally and whom she tried unsuccessfully to kill, and she became famous. Eventually she married the bartender in her Denver saloon.

H

HARDIN, JOHN WESLEY

John Wesley Hardin (1853–96), the son of a Methodist preacher, was brought up in central Texas during the post-Civil War period. He is generally regarded as one of the most notorious killers in the West, being considered a homicidal maniac. According to members of his family, his career as a killer was the result, at least in part, of trauma that he experienced when his uncle's family was massacred by a mob of Union supporters.

His first known killing involved a former slave named Mage. Hardin and Mage met at Hardin's uncle's plantation in Moscow, Texas, in November 1868 and they quarrelled over a wrestling match. Mage is said to have threatened Hardin with a stick and was shot by him. When the murder was reported to the Union army, three soldiers came to arrest Hardin but he ambushed them and killed them. These killings were suppressed by people in sympathy with the Confederates and Hardin escaped.

He then went on to a life of killing and became one of the West's legends. As with other legends, the facts are not always clear. The number of Hardin's victims is variously estimated at any number from eleven to forty-four. Although he was held to be a very good shot, he is said to have been reluctant to engage in direct confrontation.

Hardin is noted for his involvement in a family feud in De Witt County, Texas. The feud was between the Suttons and the Taylors, and Hardin intervened on the side of the Taylors, his first killing in the feud taking place in 1873. Details of the feud and Hardin's part in it are given under Sutton-Taylor feud.

In the town of Comanche in Texas, Hardin killed a sheriff. Charles Webb was pretending to be a friend of Hardin but pulled his gun to shoot him when Hardin seemed to be distracted. Hardin moved incredibly quickly and shot Webb in the head. At this point Hardin fled Texas and went to Florida and Alabama. While in Florida he was captured by John Armstrong, a Texas Ranger, and sent to prison in Huntsville, Texas. He was sentenced to twenty-five years and served sixteen, during which time he studied law. During his time in prison, also, his beloved wife died.

When he was released in 1892 he opened a law practice and moved to El Paso, Texas. Not surprisingly, clients did not flock to hire him as a lawyer and he took to drinking heavily. In August 1895 he was shot in the back of the head by John Selman, a local lawman, in a local saloon, the Acme Saloon. *See* SUTTON-TAYLOR FEUD.

HICKOK, WILD BILL

'Wild Bill' Hickok (1837–76), as he was known, was born James Butler Hickok in Homer, Illinois. He served in the Union Army during the Civil War and was for a time a spy for them. After the war he was a civilian scout for the army against the Indians. His career as a scout ended when he was thirty-one when he was badly wounded, almost fatally so, by the lance of a Cheyenne warrior.

Having gained a reputation as a frontier scout and Indian fighter, Hickok became marshal at Abilene, Kansas, when it became a booming cow town. There he encountered the notorious gunfighter Ben Thompson and his partner, Phil Coe, in the Bull's Head Saloon. Coe and Hickok took a dislike to each other and, on the night of 5 October 1871, after hearing a gunshot in the street when he was having a drink in a saloon with his friend, Mike Williams, Hickok went out and discovered that Coe had fired the shot. Coe claimed that he had fired at a dog but when asked to give up his gun pointed it at Hickok. Hickok shot him through the stomach but also accidentally shot his friend, Mike Williams.

When Hickok's contract in Abilene expired, it was not renewed. Eventually he ended up in Deadwood, South Dakota, where, in August 1876, he was shot in the back while he was playing cards by Jack McCall.

Hickok was a tall, handsome, graceful man who wore his hair long and who liked to wear fine clothes. As well as having a reputation for being exceptionally quick on the draw, he was an inveterate gambler.

Hickok is one of the great legends of the West. As with several of the other legends, it is often difficult to separate fact from fiction. The situation is further complicated by the fact that the 'legends' themselves were apt to exaggerate their exploits during their lifetime.

HOLE IN THE WALL *see* CASSIDY, BUTCH.

HOLLIDAY, DOC
John Holliday (1842–87), better known as Doc Holliday because he was a dentist by profession, was born in Georgia of an affluent family. Quite early in life he acquired a reputation as a killer, being regarded as being of a nasty disposition and having a very hot temper.

He is best known in the history and legend of the West as a friend of Wyatt Earp, being particularly remembered for his involvement with the Earp brothers at the gunfight at the OK Corral. This is dealt with in the entry on Wyatt Earp.

Holliday went to Texas from Georgia in the hope of the climate improving his health—he had contracted tuberculosis. He opened an office in Dallas and turned to gambling before going to Fort Griffin and becoming the lover of 'Big Nose' Kate Fisher, a dance-hall girl. There in January 1878 he killed a fellow gambler, Ed Bailey, in a fight over a poker game. The marshal imprisoned him in a hotel room but Kate secretly set fire to the hotel and in the ensuing panic engineered Holliday's escape.

He then went to Dodge City, Kansas, which was then becoming a boom town, and met Wyatt Earp. Holliday is credited with saving Earp's life in Dodge City in 1878. A group of cattle-rustlers ganged up on Earp in the Long Branch Saloon and the situation was looking threatening. Holliday shot one of the rustlers in the shoulder and helped escort them to jail. Wyatt Earp was everlastingly grateful.

Later Holliday joined Earp and his brothers in Tombstone, Arizona. It was there in October 1881 that the bloody gunfight at the OK Corral took place. Holliday was also involved with the Earps in the revenge for the death of Morgan Earp on Frank Stilwell and Florentino Cruz. This is dealt with in the entry on Wyatt Earp.

Holliday's tubercular condition worsened and to gain some relief he went to Glenwood Springs in Colorado. His condition deteriorated further and he died there in November 1887 at the Hotel Glenwood at the age of thirty-six. *See* EARP, WYATT.

HOMESTEAD ACT

The Homestead Act was passed in 1862 to encourage people to settle in the West. Under its provisions, a citizen over the age of twenty-one could be given the use of 160 acres of land. If he lived on it for five years and worked the land, he could claim it as his own. He could claim it as his own after six months if he were willing and able to pay $1.25 an acre for it.

At first people seemed slow to take up this offer but by the 1870s and 1880s people were rushing to take advantage of it. All manner of people decided to become homesteaders—pioneer farmers who were gradually working their way west, cowboys who had lost their jobs because of changing conditions on the ranges, war veterans and new immigrants who were anxious to make a new lives for themselves. In the ranks of the homesteaders were undoubtedly a few men who had hitherto been involved in cattle-rustling or horse-thieving.

The Homestead Act seemed a good idea to many people. Owners of large cattle ranches disagreed, however. Not only did they resent the arrival of so many people on what they had being treating as their land, resenting in particular the putting up of so many fences, but they blamed the Homestead Act for having increased the amount of rustling. Thus the Homestead Act was indirectly responsible for the vigilantism that grew up in the west and for the Range Wars. *See* RANGE WARS and VIGILANTISM.

HORN, TOM

Tom Horn (1860–1903) grew up in the Missouri area in the period after the Civil War when outlaws such as Jesse James roamed the place. He left home at the age of fourteen and worked at various jobs until he got a job as a government interpreter and scout at San Carlos reservation where some of the Apaches lived.

After his experience as a scout and interpreter, he became a miner. After that he became a Pinkerton detective in 1890 and then a range detective. He was employed in Wyoming to track and punish rustlers after the Lincoln County War.

In 1898 he returned to military service and fought in the Spanish-American War.

I

ILIFF, JOHN W.

John Iliff was the first of the cattle barons in Colorado. Born in
Ohio, he took part in the Colorado goldrush to Pike's Peak in
1859. He met with no success but, seeing the opportunities for
trade, he opened a store and, as well as supplying goods to the
miners, bartered with some of the immigrants passing through,
furnishing them with supplies in exchange for any cattle and
oxen which they might have. He turned these out on the plains
of Colorado where, to the surprise of many, they thrived. The
kind of which grew on the plain in Colorado might not look
much but it was good provender for cattle and the cattle could
winter on it as well.

There was a ready market for beef in Colorado because of the
large number of people who had gone there to seek their fortunes. Iliff was quick to capitalize on this.

His herd was made up mainly of cattle that he bought from
people who were driving their cattle north from Texas, some of
this being supplied by the partnership comprising Charles
Goodnight and Oliver Loving. It was his policy never to own
more cattle than he felt he could comfortably manage, preferring to have no more than around 40,000 head of cattle and aim-
ing for a quick turnover. The relative smallness of his herd
saved him from the worst of the cattle-rustling.

Iliff was one of the first of the cattlemen to appreciate the
value of water rights. By filing claims for water rights not only
in his own name but in the name of several of his friends and
workers, he was able to range his cattle for about 100 miles
along the Platte River. He had acquired over 30 miles of the

river frontage, his headquarters being Julesberg. Cattlemen who controlled the water were allowed to range their cows as far as they could go and still get water.

Iliff is also credited with being one of the first cattlemen to recognize the opportunities provided by ranching in Wyoming. He drove Texas cattle across the Wyoming border and in 1868 brought a slaughter herd into Cheyenne, selling some beef to local merchants and sending the rest, already butchered, to Chicago. In October of that year the first Wyoming range herd was established, the herd having been purchased in Kansas and Missouri by W. G. Bullock and B. B. Mills.

INDIANS *see* APACHES; ARAPAHO; BLACKFEET; CHEYENNE; GHOST DANCE; SIOUX; WOUNDED KNEE.

INDIAN TERRITORY

By the Indian Removal Act of 1830 passed by President Andrew Jackson, the eastern Indians were evicted from their homelands and were given in exchange a piece of virtually useless land west of the Mississippi River, which became known as Indian Territory and in time became part of Oklahoma. The Indians from the southeast, the Cherokee, the Choctaw, the Chicasaw and the Creek, were escorted there in a military trek. The idea was that the Indians who were allocated this land would be self-governing but would enjoy a certain amount of protection against, for example, land speculators or dishonest traders.

Some of the Cherokees managed to avoid the Indian Territory and escaped to the mountains of Carolina. Some of the Creeks also escaped, as did the Seminoles who were associates of the Creeks. They escaped to the Everglades in Florida

J

JAMES, FRANK
Frank James (1843-1915) was the elder brother of Jesse James and was, like him, an outlaw, being a member of the same gang. *See* JAMES, JESSE.

JAMES, JESSE
Jesse James (1847-82) was a famous outlaw who became one of the legends of the West. Born in Missouri in 1847, the son of a farmer and baptist minister, and the brother of Frank, Jesse in 1864 joined one of the guerrilla bands of William Clarke Quantrill, the band being led by 'Bloody Bill' Anderson. The James family had aligned themselves with the Confederate side on the start of the Civil War, being in fact slave-owners, and Quantrill had also aligned himself with the Confederate side. Frank james had joined Quantrill in 1863 and both he and Jesse were to learn much about murder and destruction from people who were experts in the field.

Surrender and injury
At Centralia in Missouri, Jesse alongside Anderson participated in the killing of twenty-four Union soldiers who were unarmed. When the end of the Civil War was obviously in sight, Jesse James attempted to surrender under cover of a white flag at Lexington. The Union forces, however, rejected this attempt at surrender, since James had not been an official participator in the war but a member of a guerilla force. Instead they shot him, seriously wounding him in his right lung. At one point he was close to death but he recovered.

There was much bitterness in the south at the end of the war. A great many men were demobilized but had got used to war and were still looking for trouble. The James brothers had got used to trouble and violence in their guerilla bands and seemed anxious to continue with such a way of life.

The Liberty bank raid

Because the James brothers became such legends, it is often quite difficult to establish which of the information circulating about the James brothers was fact and which was fiction. The raid on the Clay County Saving Association Bank on 13 February 1866 is a case in point. Some sources indicate that both brothers were definitely there and even that Jesse at least played a major part. Others indicate that this is more doubtful, suggesting that Frank was probably and that Jesse may have been. There is some speculation that the leader of the raid was Arch Clement, a good friend of Frank James and a notorious killer, and that Cole Younger was also present.

Whatever the case, it was the kind of event with which they became very familiar. When most of the townspeople of Liberty were in the courthouse watching a trial, a gang of armed robbers entered the Clay County Saving Association Bank and held it up. They took the money and shot the only bystander outside the bank.

Sympathy for outlaws

Thereafter there were a serious of bank raids in some of which the James brothers appeared, although they were not yet leaders. Because the local farmers and businessmen regarded the local bankers as mean people who would not lend them the money that they needed to restore their farms and properties after the ravages of war, they certainly did not have friendly feelings towards banks and bankers. Instead they felt some sympathy with the people who were robbing the bankers, although a lynching of some of the robbers who attacked a bank at Richmond was clearly not carried out by people of such a frame of mind.

Russelville

In March 1868 Jesse James planned a bank raid on the Norton-Long Bank in Russelville, Kentucky, although he was not present at the actual raid. The robbers got the money but they had to fight their way through a band of townspeople who had been alerted by the bank's elderly president. George Shepherd, one of the gang members lived to regret his presence there because a detective hired by the bank tracked him down and he was sent to prison for three years.

Gallatin

His fate clearly did not worry the other members of the gang. In December 1869 the James brothers raided the Davies County Bank at Gallatin, Missouri. This appears to have been the first robbery in which the James brothers were positively identified as being present, although Jesse James in a letter to the *Kansas City Times* denied that he had been there and claimed to be a peaceable, law-abiding citizen.

Soon after that the James brothers teamed up with the Younger brothers to commit robbery and murder from Alabama to Iowa for about ten years. Banks were raided and trains and stagecoaches were held up, with anyone who got in the way being killed.

Audacity

The tales of robbery and murder also include tales of audacity and impudence. One such centres on the robbing of a bank at Corydon in Iowa. After the raid when the James-Younger gang had taken the money from the bank, they rode to the local church where a political meeting was in progress. Jesse shouted that they had robbed the bank and they rode off.

Death of Archie Samuel

The year 1874 was the year in which the activities of the James gang reached a peak and their catalogue of crimes, robbing trains, stagecoaches, banks, stores, and even a steamboat, is phenomenal. Tragedy, however, was round the corner. In January 1875 one of the Pinkerton detectives, Jack Ladd, thought that he had caught sight of the James brothers at the house of their mother. She was by this time known as Mrs Zerelda Samuel, having married Dr Reuben Samuel after the death of the boys' father in 1850.

That night her house in Clay County was surrounded by detectives hired by the banks and railroad companies to track the robbers down. They tossed into the house what they claim was a flare to enable them to see their targets better and what the James family claimed was a grenade. The tragedy of the device did not centre on Jesse and Frank James but on their half-brother, Archie Samuel. He was killed by a fragment from the metal casing of the device and Mrs Samuel's forearm was injured so badly that it had to be amputated.

Mrs Samuel claimed that Jesse and Frank were not even at home that night. Because of the involvement of a child there was much feeling against the detectives and much sympathy for the James brothers.

Northfield bank raid

Good fortune, however, was not with the Jameses yet. They and the Youngers planned a raid on a bank in Northfield, Minnesota. It was farther north than they usually ventured but their usual territory was full of detectives and lawmen eager to claim the reward money offered for members of the gang. The Northfield raid went horribly wrong. One of the bank tellers was able to escape and raise the alarm. The people of Northfield grabbed what weapons they could, had a running battle with the gang and went off in pursuit of them when they fled.

Several of the gang had been injured in the fracas at the bank and two of them were killed. One of the injured was Bob Younger and in addition his horse was felled. The James brothers wanted to abandon him so that they could escape more quickly but Cole Younger refused. There was a quarrel and the James brothers parted company with the rest. They escaped and got back safely to Missouri. The Younger brothers and the rest were not so lucky but the rest of their story appears under the entry at Younger brothers.

Law-abiding lives
Both the James boys had got married in 1874, Jesse to his cousin Zerelda Mimms and Frank to Annie Ralton, a farmer's daughter. For more than three years after the Northfield debacle the James brothers lived quietly under assumed names with their families, at first in Tennessee, where Jesse James's two children were born. Jesse James had adopted the name of J D Howard.

Back to a life of crime
This was too good to last, and in 1879 the James gang robbed the Chicago and Alton Railroad train at Glendale Station in Missouri and two years later the gang murdered two men during the hold-up of a train at Winston, Missouri. A reward was put up for the capture of Jesse and Frank James.

Death for Jesse
The size of the reward, $10,000, was too much for one member of the James gang, and Bob Ford agreed to kill Jesse James for

the reward money. The story of the killing is told in the entry under Bob Ford.

Frank James
Six months after the death of Jesse in April 1882, Frank surrendered and was tried on several charges. The public sympathy that had always been in evidence for the James brothers and perhaps the fear of reprisals ensured that he was not convicted. He then spent some time shooting the starter pistol at country fairs and charging visitors 50 cents to see round the James house. He dabbled with Cole Younger in running a wild west show and joined with him in giving talks on the evils of crime.

Frank died in 1915. *See* FORD, BOB and YOUNGER BROTHERS.

JA RANCH *see* ADAIR, JOHN and GOODNIGHT, CHARLES.

JOHNSON COUNTY WAR
The Johnson County War was a confrontation between the 'Regulators', a secret society formed by the Wyoming Stock Growers' Association, which was in effect a vigilante gang. They were formed under the leadership of Major Frank Wolcott, who got together an army of gunmen. Their aim was to stamp out rustling among the homesteaders of Wyoming. With this in mind, Wolcott was given a list of homesteaders and rustlers who were to be executed for what the Regulators perceived as their criminal activities. Frank Canton, who knew Johnson County better than any of the Regulators, was persuaded at a price to come from Chicago to Cheyenne, Wyoming, in order to help with the military-style campaign of lynchings.

Wolcott, Canton, the hired gunmen, some of the members of the Regulators, Charles Penrose, the official surgeon to the party, and two journalists, one from Cheyenne and one from Chicago, who went along as war correspondents, set out. Wolcott even hired a special train from the Union Pacific Railroad in Denver. The train was loaded at Cheyenne with weapons, ammunition, dynamite, tents, blankets, wagons, horses, and supplies.

On the morning of 7 April 1892, the army arrived at the end of the railroad line in Casper. The army of vigilantes immediately cut the telegraph wires to Buffalo. They set out on horseback towards Buffalo, having sent some scouts on ahead. It was apparently their intention to go straight to Buffalo and publicly hang the sheriff, Bill 'Red' Angus.

KC Ranch

However, they had a change of plan. While the army had stopped for a rest at the ranch of Bob Tisdale, who was a member of the party, it was brought to Wolcott's attention by one of the scouts that two of the people on his extermination list were wintering at KC Ranch. The two men were Nick Ray and Nate Champion. Immediately Wolcott decided to make a detour.

At the KC Ranch, Ray and Champion had two guests, two trappers, Bill Walker and Ben Jones. When the two trappers went outside they were immediately and silently captured so that there was no possibility of giving any warning to their friends inside.

Nick Ray came out to find out what had happened to the trappers when they did not return. He was instantly fired at by the Regulators' gang and was badly wounded. As he began to try to crawl back indoors, Champion ran out and began to pull him inside by his collar, firing with his other hand.

Champion, a Texan like many of the hired gunmen in the Regulators' gang, put up a magnificent fight against overwhelming odds. He succeeded in holding off his attackers for several hours, although Nick Ray had died of his wounds. Champion even found time during the crossfire to write an account of his experiences.

About three o'clock in the afternoon two men had ridden by the ranch. They were Jack Flag, a homesteader and editor from Buffalo, and his stepson, who was driving a wagon. The two were alarmed by the gunfire and rode as fast as they could towards Buffalo to raise the alarm.

Death of Champion

Meanwhile, the Regulators piled an old wagon with hay and brushwood and set fire to it before pushing it against Champion's cabin. Champion had no choice but to come out. He decided to make a dash for it and tried to run for cover but he was shot at by about twenty rifles. Although he fired back he was hopelessly outnumbered and he was soon dead.

Before riding off, his killers found his notebook with the account of the attack and erased with a knife the name he had included, thought to be Canton. They then replaced the notebook and pinned a placard to Champion's coat saying 'Cattle thieves beware!'

Opposition

By this time word of the attack had reached Sheriff Angus, who was himself on the Regulators' hit list. He was quickly forming an opposing army and within a few hours he had a few hundred men. They rode out of Buffalo and were spotted by one of the Regulators' scout. He quickly rode back to warn Wolcott and his men who were about fourteen miles south of Buffalo. The Regulators had a quick change of plan and retreated to the TA Ranch on Crazy Woman Creek where they had halted a short time before.. There they barricaded themselves in and prepared for a siege.

TA Ranch

The battle of the TA Ranch began on 11 April. The Buffalo contingent was by this time under the leadership of Arapaho

Brown, Sheriff Angus having returned to Buffalo to sort things out there. Towards the end of the second day Arapaho Brown decided to build a device that would get the Regulators and their gang out of the ranch. The device was similar to the wagon of burning hay with which the Regulators had got Champion out of the KC Ranch. They were just preparing such a device using dynamite when, just like something out of a clichéd western film, the cavalry arrived under the leadership of Colonel J. J. Van Horn.

During the previous evening, Wolcott had succeeded in secretly getting a scout out of the TA Ranch to take a message to the Wyoming Stock Growers' Association. The Association then got in touch with Amos Barber who was Acting Governor at the time. He sent a message urging President Harrison to send troops to relieve the besieged Regulators.

Surrender

Wolcott agreed to surrender to Van Horn although not to the Buffalo unofficial army. Colonel Van Horn refused to turn over the Regulators to Sheriff Angus, knowing that they would probably be lynched. Instead the Regulators were taken to Fort DA Russell where the expenses for their guards and food was charged to Johnson County while they awaited trial.

Freedom

The Regulators should have been found guilty of murder. However, for various reasons they went free. The trappers who had been at the KC Ranch should have been produced as witnesses but they were scared for their lives and accepted bribes to flee the state. No jurors acceptable to both sides could be found, and Johnson County had empty coffers from having had to maintain the Regulators in Fort DA Russell and had no money for what would undoubtedly be a lengthy prosecution.

In January 1893 the Regulators were allowed to go free. Although they were never prosecuted for their terrible deeds, the powerful stockmen did lose a great deal of their power and it was clear that the days of the open range were numbered. The Wyoming stockmen were, however, reluctant to admit this and were still determined to put an end to rustling. They thus took to employing Tom Horn, a former range detective, to murder people whom they suspected of cattle-thieving.

Nate Champion became one of the heroes of the West. Indeed, partly thanks to his written account of the attack on him, he became one of the great heroes of the frontier *See* HORN, TOM.

JOSEPH, CHIEF

Chief Joseph was a chief of the Nez Perces. He was originally named Hin-mah-too-yah-lat-kekht or Thunder Rolling from the Mountains. Of the Indian peoples, the Nez Perces had one of the best relationships with the white men for a long time. In 1836 they had welcomed missionaries such as Henry and Eliza Spalding. The missionaries had a good deal of success with establishing small missions, resulting in a number of conversions and a number changes of name—hence Joseph.

In 1877 the friendship between Joseph and the Nez Perces and the white men was put to a harsh test when the white men demanded that the Nez Perces land be handed over them and the Nez Perces go to live in a reservation at Lapwai in Idaho. If the Nez Perces refused they would be removed forcibly from their land and compelled to go to the reservation.

Joseph had promised his father, also called Joseph, that he would never give the Nez Perces land to the white men and that he would take care not to be cheated by the white men out of the land. Joseph senior had insisted that a line of demarcation be drawn between the white people's territory and the territory of the Nez Perces, this territory being in the Wallowa Valley, also known as the Valley of Winding Waters.

In 1863 Joseph the younger, now a chief following the death of his father, had refused to sign a treaty by which Joseph and his people would leave the Wallowa Valley and go to live in a reservation. The government took no action against him but cattle ranchers began to graze their herds on the land belonging to the Nez Perces. Goldminers were also beginning to arrive.

In 1868 several Indian leaders, including two other chiefs of the Nez Perces, went to Washington to sign a treaty agreeing to withdraw to reservations and give up their land. Chief Joseph refused to go to Washington and refused to have anything to do with such a treaty. In 1873 President Ulysses Grant issued an order confirming that Wallowa valley belonged to the Nez Perces. Many of the white settlers were furious at not being allowed to use the land.

In 1875 President Grant gave into public pressure and reversed his ruling and allowed white settlers on to Wallowa valley. General Howard of the Department of Columbia tried to persuade Washington to confirm Chief Joseph's claim to the land. Washington refused and violent incidents began to take place.

In 1876 the authorities once again asked Joseph to give up the land and go to the reservation in Lapwai. Once again he refused and in 1877 he was ordered to go peaceably with his people to the reservation or force would be used against him. Reluctantly Chief Joseph agreed to accept the demands of the whites because he did not want to engage in a war.

Some of the other members of the Nez Perces leadership were not in favour of Chief Joseph's decision and called him a coward. Without Joseph's knowledge, a few braves slipped away and attacked some white people, and General Howard's soldiers under Colonel David Perry attacked the Nez Perces camp at White Bird Canyon on 17 June 1877. The troops were routed by the Indians and a number of them were killed. When

General Howard brought reinforcements they too were routed.

Realizing that they were hopelessly outnumbered as more troops arrived, Chief Joseph and the other Nez Perces leaders decided to try to escape to Canada, where Sitting Bull of the Sioux had gone, or at least to Montana. They thought that General Howard would not bother to follow them but his soldiers kept after them. The Indians succeeded in winning three battles against the American troops while they were still in Idaho.

Having travelled peacefully through part of Montana, the Nez Perces decided to rest at a place called the Big Hole. On 9 August tragedy struck for them . General Gibbon attacked when the Indians were asleep. Many women and children were killed as well as some warriors. The surviving warriors fought back and drove the soldiers from their camp.

The Nez Perces kept travelling and the troops kept following them. After a few skirmishes the Nez Perces met a troop of Cavalry under Colonel Samuel Sturgis at Canyon Creek. The Indians won but had very few fighting men left.

Chief Joseph and his people continued to make for Canada but on 29 September they once again had to do battle—against General Miles at Bear Paw. The Indians fought bravely but the weather was very cold and the battle turned into a siege. General Miles told Chief Joseph that if he surrendered he could return home. In view of the state of his people who had been travelling for so long, Joseph agreed, although some of his men escaped and got to Canada.

The government did not honour the promise given by General Miles, and the Nez Perces under Chief Joseph were sent to a reservation in the Indian Territory in what is now Oklahoma. The Wallowa Valley had been, dry, cool and pleasant and the Indian Territory was hot, humid and disease-ridden. Many of the Nez Perces died and some committed suicide.

Chief Joseph went to Washington and impressed many people

with an impassioned speech about the importance of treating all people the same. Many people argued that Joseph and his people should be allowed to return to their own land but the white settlers there were nervous of that suggestion and Joseph and his people stayed put in the Indian Territory.

In 1885 some of the Nez Perces were allowed to go the reservation in Idaho. However, Chief Joseph and about 150 others were sent to a reservation in Washington to live among some other Indian peoples who were not too friendly towards the Nez Perces.

Chief Joseph died in the reservation in 1904. For the rest of his life he had argued eloquently to achieve peaceful freedom for the Nez Perces and other Indian peoples but in vain.

K

KANSAS
Kansas features in the history of the Wild West largely because of the cow towns. *See* ABILENE; COW TOWN; DODGE CITY; ELLSWORTH and WICHITA.

KELTON, ELMER
Elmer Kelton is a Texan novelist who writes historical fiction often based on events in Texas. They have a realism that a lot of other novels about the West lack and they contrast sharply with the many novels about the West that present a romanticized, stylized picture of the cowboys' way of life.

His novels include *The Time It Never Rained* (1973), *The Good Old Boys* (1978) and *The Man Who Rode Midnight* (1987).

L

L'AMOUR, LOUIS

Louis L'Amour (1908–1988) was a novelist who specialized in western fiction. He was the most prolific of all writers of pulp western fiction and had sold more than 200 million books by the time he died. His novels were romantic and action-packed and did not present a true, realistic picture of life in the west, although L'Amour, himself, boasted of the historical grounding of his books.

LEWIS AND CLARK EXPEDITION

The Lewis and Clark expedition was so called because the leaders of the expedition were Captain Meriwether Lewis (1774–1809) and William Clark (1770–1838). They were both from Virginia and were friends and army colleagues.

Lewis was asked by President Thomas Jefferson to put together and lead an expedition that would make its way along the Missouri River and go farther west to try to discover a link between the Mississippi and the Pacific. Lewis in turn requested that Clark be co-leader and Jefferson agreed.

Purchase of Louisiana

Jefferson was able to order this expedition because he had negotiated a deal with Napoleon Bonaparte by which America bought Louisiana from the French. Jefferson had wanted New Orleans because of its importance in controlling the Mississippi but Bonaparte offered the entire territory and Jefferson agreed. The as yet uncharted territory of Louisiana was to be charted.

The expedition

The expedition was also to record anything noteworthy about

the flora, fauna and topography of the land through which it passed. Also to be noted was anything relevant to the people who lived in the area—way of life, customs and traditions, and so on. It was an onerous task but it was in capable hands.

Lewis and Clark selected thirty experienced soldiers and frontiersmen with a wide range of skills for their 'Corps of Discovery' and set off on 14 May 1804 with a 60-foot keelboat, several smaller boats, and gifts and trade goods for any Indians whom they met, as well as enough provisions for two years of travel. Clark was responsible for navigation and mapping, and Lewis was responsible for observing and noting natural phenomena and for collecting specimens of native flora.

Sacajawea

They had some encounters with Indians but these were all in the end negotiated peacefully. Setting up a winter camp in what is now Dakota among the friendly Mandan Indians, the expedition took on a new recruit, a fur trapper named Toussaint Charbonneau and his sixteen-year-old wife, Sacajawea, and baby. Sacajawea was of the Shoshoni Indian tribe and had been captured as a child by the Hidatsa Indians. She was to prove extremely useful to the expedition.

When the ice broke up on the Missouri River in March, the keelboat was sent back to St Louis with the expedition records to date and the specimens that had been collected. The rest of the party headed upriver. When they reached the Great Falls of the Missouri, they faced a twenty-five-day walk to avoid the rapids, carrying their equipment and provisions.

Shoshonis

When they reached the foothills of the Rocky Mountains, they hoped to meet the Shoshonis and acquire horses from them to enable them to cross the mountains, a very gruelling part of the trip. Sacajawea was instrumental in directing Lewis and a small band to a Shoshoni village although they had difficulty in finding it and had to capture two Shoshoni women to show them the way. Lewis persuaded some of the Indians to accompany his group back to meet the main party. The Shoshoni were reluctant but eventually their chief, Cameahwait, went with Lewis. He was delighted to discover that Sacajawea was there as she was his long-lost sister.

The Shoshonis supplied the members of the expedition with horses and they set off over the Rocky Mountains, on their arduous journey. At the mouth of Lolo Creek, in present-day Montana, they went west in appallingly cold and wet conditions and reached the territory of the Nez Perces Indians to whom they gave their horses.

Pacific

They built dugout canoes and negotiated rapids until they reached the Snake River. This they followed until they reached the Columbia. Finally they reached the Pacific on 15 November 1805. They were exhausted and hungry, with nothing to eat but roots and dried fish, but were obviously delighted to have done what they had set out to do.

Return

The members of the expedition built a fort, which they named Fort Clatsop after a local Indian tribe, and wintered there. They retraced their route as far as Lolo Creek and then split into two groups. Clark explored the Yellowstone River. Lewis with a small group went directly across country to the Falls of Missouri. The two groups met in St Louis, Missouri, on 23 September 1806.

Opening up of the west

The journey had been extremely successful, with the loss of only one life, that of Sergeant Charles Flyod. They did not discover a Northwest Passage because such a thing did not exist but it charted around 8,000 miles of previously unknown territory and discovered many hitherto unknown species of plants, birds and animals. It also reported the presence of beaver, which was to encourage fur-trappers to migrate west and begin the early opening up of the west.

Lewis and Clark

Of the two leaders, Clark went on to have a distinguished career as the first Superintendent of Indian Affairs, having acquired much skill in dealing with the Native American Indians in the course of the expedition. Lewis did not have such a happy career. In 1809, while he was on his way to Washington to edit the journals relating to the expedition, he died of pistol wounds in a cabin in Tennessee. Whether he was murdered or whether he committed suicide is not known.

LINCOLN COUNTY WAR

Lincoln County was a large area located in the southeast of New Mexico. The population was partly American, partly Mexican and partly Indian. The origins of the Lincoln County War are complex.

Two Civil War veterans, Major Laurence Murphy, of Irish extraction, and Emil Fritz, of German extraction, started a store in Lincoln County and this became known as the House. They were joined by James Dolan and John Riley. They also ran cattle on the ranges and supplied the Apache reservation in the county and the troops at Fort Stanton with beef. They were good friends with the sheriff, William Brady, and the Santa Fe Ring, a group of businessmen and politicians in Santa Fe who were regarded as being unscrupulous.

Murphy and his associates were much disliked and much distrusted. They were felt to be corrupt and to be forcing others to take a low price for their cattle and to buy goods at inflated prices. In particular, people were unhappy about their association with the sheriff.

John Chisum

The ambitious Texan Murphy and his associate, however, had competition in their efforts to control the region. John Chisum was the owner of a large ranch along the Pecos River. He had been a trail-driver and a meat-packer and had amassed a very large herd of Longhorns. Consequently he was an easy target for rustlers. Even when he did succeed in catching the elusive rustlers, they always seemed to escape prosecution.

Alexander McSween

It would be difficult to prove but Chisum was convinced that Murphy was responsible for the rustling of his cattle and that Murphy's friendship with the sheriff was responsible for the fact that it was difficult to prosecute the rustlers. Indeed, Chisum was so convinced that Murphy was behind the rustling of his cattle that he accused him directly. Murphy denied the whole thing contemptuously, but he employed a young Scots-Canadian lawyer, Alexander McSween, to represent him.

One day Chisum's men caught Murphy's men red-handed and McSween refused to defend them in the light of the blatant evidence. Chisum then retained McSween to represent his legal interests. Murphy was furious at this change of loyalties.

John Tunstall

Chisum had a third man on his side. An Englishman named Tunstall had been attracted to the West by romantic tales of its wildness. He was very British in his ways but he soon won the respect of his workers and the neighbouring ranchers. He arrived in 1876 and set up a ranch and opened a store. He appointed McSween to manage his business. Meanwhile Chisum opened a bank with Tunstall's help at the back of the Tunstall-McSween building and Murphy was very annoyed.

Dispute

Then McSween fell out with Murphy on the details of Fritz's will, Murphy claiming that all the assets of the estate were his. He then had McSween charged with embezzlement of these assets. McSween transferred his property to Tunstall.

Murphy was already jealous of Tunstall's success with his ranch and his store, which was providing significant competition for Murphy's House, and this transference of property annoyed him further. He decided to take action against both McSween and Tunstall and arranged for Sheriff Brady, who was a good friend of his, to take a posse and go to Tunstall's property and seize cattle to the value of what Murphy felt he was owed.

Death of Tunstall

In February 1878 William Brady and the posse showed up on Tunstall's ranch. The deputies were armed and the posse is also said to have included some outlaws specially recruited for the occasion. There are various versions of what happened then. Some say that Tunstall was not at the ranch, that the armed posse went out looking for him and that Tunstall's party was ambushed on the Lincoln road, Tunstall being mortally wounded by a bullet in the chest. Brady reported that he had been killed because he resisted arrest.

The fact that Tunstall was killed is common to all the versions of the story. One of these indicates that Tunstall was present when Brady and his armed posse arrived at his ranch and that with great reluctance he went with Brady to town, accompanied by some of his ranch-hands. It also indicates that Murphy claimed that Tunstall may have fired first and was killed by a return shot but others claim that he was shot in the back.

Billy the Kid

The feeling between Chisum and McSween on one side and Murphy on the other was more hostile than ever. A new character now entered the fray. This was a young man calling himself William Bonney. In fact, unknown to everyone, he was the notorious outlaw, Billy the Kid.

He had appeared in Lincoln County in 1877 just as the situation between Chisum and Murphy was reaching boiling point. It is not absolutely clear how he managed to be working as a ranch-hand for Tunstall. It has been suggested that he first began his career in Lincoln County by working as part of a gang that was raiding Chisum's herds but that he gave that up to work for Frank Coe, who owned a small ranch in the area. He was a neighbour of Dick Brewer, who not only had his own small ranch but acted as manager to Tunstall. Brewer in turn is said to have introduced William Bonney to Tunstall, who hired him as a ranch-hand/gunman in his struggle against Murphy.

However he came to meet Tunstall, William Bonney became a member of Tunstall's staff in January 1878 and developed a respect and admiration for his boss. This was to prove a factor in the bloody events of the Lincoln County War.

Some of the cattlemen of Lincoln County decided that they had better join McSween and Chisum against Murphy in view of what had happened to Tunstall. Tempers were set to run very high.

Capture and death of Tunstall's killers

It was decided that a posse should be sent to bring to trial the men who had been responsible for Tunstall's death. Brewer, who was a kind of special constable, was in charge. They had decided that there was no point in asking Sheriff Brady to arrest the men in view of his friendship with Murphy.

The McSween supporters captured Billy Morton, believed to

be the actual killer of Tunstall, and Frank Baker. They stopped overnight at Chisum's ranch with their captives and heard that Murphy's men had sent out a posse to get the men back. The McSween supporters thought that Murphy's men would prevent the men from going to trial and so they shot them themselves. Some sources indicate that the men were killed when trying to escape.

More killings followed, among them that of Sheriff Brady, killed by Billy the Kid, and a deputy, and Dick Brewer, leader of the McSween group. The war carried on relentlessly throughout 1878, with much bloodshed.

Battle

Things came to a head in July when there was a pitched battle between the two sides. McSween and his wife with some of his men were in his house and they were surrounded. Anxious to prevent any more bloodshed, McSween asked for talks to take place but Murphy's men refused. The battle raged for three days and then a company of infantrymen and a troop of cavalrymen under the command of Colonel Nathan Dudley arrived, complete with Gatling gun and twelve-pound cannon.

McSween explained to Dudley that he had tried to stop the fighting and that he and his men were simply defending themselves. Dudley explained that the new sheriff, George Peppin, had told him that McSween and his men were outside the law and as such could not be defended by the troops. He ordered them to stop firing.

Fire and death

Meanwhile some of Murphy's men had gone round the back of McSween's house and set fire to the back porch as Dudley's troop moved off. Soon the fire was raging and two men were killed trying to escape. To save further bloodshed, McSween offered to give himself up but he was shot dead on the doorstep.

Others were also killed when they made a break from the burning house, but William Bonney and some of the others escaped.

Now McSween was dead and Tunstall had been dead for some time. Major Murphy was also dead, although he had not died in the conflict. He had died peacefully of natural causes in hospital before the final battle had begun. It did prove to be the last battle of the Lincoln County War. Chisum then lost interest in the feud with the rest of the main contenders gone.

Billy the Kid, however, did not lose interest. He and some of his gang were still determined to take vengeance on all those who had been involved in the killing of Tunstall and now there was McSween's death to be avenged as well.

The rest of the story of Billy the Kid is to be found under Billy the Kid. *See* BILLY THE KID.

LONGBAUGH *or* **LONGABAUGH, HARRY** *see* SUNDANCE KID.

LOVING, OLIVER
Oliver Loving was the partner of Charles Goodnight and he joined him in his trailblazing and cattle-driving. Loving, however, did not have such a long career as Goodnight. He and a friend, Bill Wilson, were attacked in 1867 by a Comanche war party. Wilson managed to escape to go for help when Loving was wounded in the arm by a Comanche arrow and had a horrendous journey until he met Goodnight. When they got to where Wilson had left Loving, he was not there and he assumed that he was dead.

However, Loving had managed to withstand the Comanche siege and also survived several days of wandering, practically starving to death, until he was found and taken to Fort Sumner. There it was found that his arm had turned gangrenous and the only doctor there amputated it. However, the operation was not a success and he died. *See* GOODNIGHT, CHARLES.

LYNCHING

Lynching refers to the practice of condemning and putting to death a suspect without giving him or her the benefit of a trial. This summary form of punishment was often carried out by the vigilante groups of the west, often against people who were suspected of cattle-rustling. Favourite methods used by the vigilantes included hanging people from branches of trees or tying people to trees and setting fire to them. *See* VIGILANTISM.

M

McCOY, JOSEPH

Joseph McCoy (1837–1915) was a cattle-dealer from Illinois who pioneered the Texan cattle trade with Kansas and was responsible for the success of the first of the booming Kansas cow towns. He conceived the idea of building a sales yard and railhead at Abilene, at that time just a hamlet but a hamlet near a railroad line. McCoy had difficulty in persuading Kansas Pacific Railroad to be interested in the project and to build the required switchline but at last he succeeded.

McCoy had purchased a tract of land there, and in July 1867 began to build a shipping yard, a barn, an office and a hotel, allowing himself sixty days for this task. Meanwhile he had sent his friend, William Sugg, south to Texas to tell cattlemen about the new arrangement.

There was already a suitable cattle trail in existence. This ran directly from Kansas through Indian Territory to Red River and into Texas. The trail was named Chisholm Trail after a Cherokee-Scots trader who had used the trail to transport goods south in 1864 and to transport buffalo hides and some cattle in 1865, returning north along the trail to mark the road more clearly. The trail had been earlier used by a Delaware scout called Black Beaver to guide goldrush expeditions and to guide soldiers to safety from the Indian Territory at the outbreak of the Civil War. All McCoy had to do was to extend the trail from Wichita, where it ended, to Abilene.

The Texas cattlemen were all too eager to find a market in the east and north for their stock. Hitherto the nearest railroad point for Texans wishing to ship cattle was Sedalia, Missouri, but the journey was fraught with obstacles. The Indians demanded tolls for passing cattle through their land, and from Baxter Springs in Kansas to Sedalia the Texans had to face the new settlers, known as Jayhawkers, who were farmers who did not wish their fences wrecked and their crops destroyed by cattle. In addition they did not wish to have their stock affected by Spanish fever or Texan fever, which affected Texan cattle. In fact, this was spread by ticks but they did not know that then. Finally, many of the Jayhawkers had no love for the Texans, as many of them had been on different sides in the Civil War.

Abilene, then, became popular with the Texan cattlemen and became a boom town. However, as the railway pushed westwards the success of Abilene waned as other cow towns prospered. McCoy sold his land in Abilene and became involved in projects in the other cow towns, such as Newtown and Wichita.

MANGAS COLORADOS

Mangas Colorados, 'Red Sleeves', was one of the great Apache chiefs, a chief of the Chiricahua. The Apache were a mountain people who were native to Arizona and New Mexico. At first they lived in relative peace with the white men, even when the latter began to prospect for gold and silver in their lands. However, the treatment of Mangas Colorados in the late 1850s at the hands of the white men changed the peaceful attitude of the Apache.

In the late 1850s Mangas Colorados made a visit to Pinos Altos in the southwest of New Mexico. He went in peace and was friendly to the miners there. They, however, vastly insulted not only Mangas himself but the whole Apache people by tying the chief to a tree and lashing him into a state of unconsciousness with a bullwhip. Naturally he was very angry and appealed for help to the great Apache warrior chief Cochise to help him avenge the insult. It was the end of peace with the whites for some time.

Mangas Colorados was injured in the Apache Pass ambush in 1862. He was wounded in the chest and, although it was not fatal, it made him realize that he was tired of warfare. The following year he decided to go alone to Pinos Altos and take up the American authorities' offer of peace. Brevet General Joseph West ordered Mangas to be seized and let it be known to the guards that he wanted the Apache chief dead.

The guards then began heating their bayonets in the fire and burning the chief's feet and legs. When Mangas protested, they shot him dead, afterwards scalping and decapitating him. The white men in their defence said that he had been resisting arrest.

Naturally the ill-treatment and death of Mangas Colorados made Cochise and the rest of the Apaches even more reluctant to make peace with the white men. *See* APACHES; COCHISE and GERONIMO.

MASTERSON, WILLIAM B. ('BAT')

Bat Masterson (1853–1921), born in Canada and the brother of Edward Masterson, was a lawman and gunfighter. He was sheriff of Ford County when his brother Edward was marshal of Dodge City. He had made his name as a buffalo hunter, scout, Indian-fighter—he had been at the battle of Adobe Walls in 1874—and a gunfighter before taking up the appointment at Ford County, although his reputation as a gunfighter and killer is thought to have been much exaggerated, not least by himself. In this way he has become part of the myth of the violent West.

At Ford County he led a posse that was responsible for arresting most of a gang that had held up a train near Dodge City. He left Ford County in 1880 to take up a variety of jobs elsewhere, becoming among other things a fight-promoter. He ended his career and life at the sports desk of a New York paper.

He is noted not only for his skill as a gunman but also as the giver of advice as to what constitutes a good gunman. He is quoted as saying, 'Any man who does not possess courage, proficiency in the use of firearms, and deliberation had better make up his mind at the beginning to settle his differences in some other manner than by appeal to the pistol.'

MAVERICK

The name given in the West to an unbranded calf. In spring on the range it was quite common to find calves that did not have an identifiable mother. Calves were marked with the brand that had been used on their mothers but obviously this was not possible where the mother was not known. Unbranded calves were often assumed to be orphans and a maverick calf could be claimed by whoever found it. This practice, of course, left room for people to abuse the system and some cowboys were accused of branding as their own calves that were not orphans but which the owner had not yet branded.

MAVERICK ACT

An act secured by cattle barons in Wyoming that made it illegal for anyone who was not a member of the Stock Grower's Association to brand an unbranded—or maverick—calf. *See* WYOMING STOCK GROWERS' ASSOCIATION.

MAXWELL, KATE

Kate Maxwell was the alias of Ella Watson, business partner of

Jim Averill, who, with him, was lynched for suspected rustling or acceptance of maverick cattle. *See* AVERILL, JIM and WATSON, ELLA.

MORMONS
The Mormons had a significant effect on the West because of their mass migration west from Nauvoo, Illinois, under the leadership of Brigham Young. The first of the Mormons started off from the east in 1846 and arrived in the Salt Lake area in 1847.

The vision of Joseph Smith
The Mormon movement had its origins in New York state in 1827 when a young man claimed that he had had a vision in which he was visited by the angel Moroni. The young man was Joseph Smith, and he claimed that the angel revealed to him the whereabouts of some golden tablets that contained some hitherto missing parts of the Bible, which became known as the Book of Mormon. Joseph Smith was illiterate but a pair of magic spectacles was thoughtfully included with the written material and these enabled Smith to read and interpret the message imparted by it.

The relevant message supposedly imparted by the missing parts of the Bible was that two of the lost tribes of Israel had found their way to America. These were the Lamanites and the Nephites. The Lamanites were depicted as being cruel and wicked and supposedly killed the Nephites, except for one man called Mormon who lived long enough to write the story in hieroglyphics on the golden tablets. According to Smith, it was indicated that the Lamanites were the forefathers of the native American Indians.

The Church of Jesus Christ of the Latter-Day Saints
Joseph Smith published *The Book of Mormon* in 1830. He then

founded the Church of Jesus Christ of the Latter-Day Saints on
6 June of the same year at Fayette. He was persuasive and had a
flair for recruiting converts. Nonbelievers in the area, however,
showed their hostility to Smith and his converts, and he decided
to move his followers to Kirtland in Ohio. Missionaries were
sent out and a thousand converts were recruited, among them
Brigham Young who was to replace Joseph Smith as leader of
the Mormons on his death.

On the move

The Mormons were very industrious and soon had a thriving
community with their own store, bank, mill and printing press
in Kirtland. The people of Kirtland were deeply suspicious of,
and resentful of, these clannish people in their midst, and tarred
and feathered Smith.

Smith decided that it was time to move on again. The chosen
site was Independence, Missouri, but again the Mormons met
with strong opposition. Pitched battles occurred, the militia
were called out against the Mormons and then nineteen Mormon men and boys were killed.

Clearly it was time to move on. This time the Mormons
moved to Nauvoo in Illinois. There, with the industry that had
come to typify them, they built a populous city from what was a
swamp. At first the city was virtually an independent state but
the outside world intervened when a group of Mormon dissent-
ers fled to Carthage in Illinois.

Imprisonment and death for Joseph Smith

They confirmed what was already being rumoured there—that
Smith was advocating and practising polygamy, having claimed
that he had had a call from God to end monogamy. There was
uproar and the authorities issued warrants for the arrest of
Joseph Smith and his brother Hyrum. Smith placed Nauvoo un-

der martial law but surrendered himself to the authorities at Carthage on 24 June 1844.

Smith is said to have had a premonition when he entered the Carthage jail. Events proved that his premonition was justified and he and Hyrum were shot by a mob of masked people who stormed the jail.

Migration west with Brigham Young

The death of Smith meant a further move for the Mormons. Under the leadership of Brigham Young they migrated west, it being Young's feeling that they should seek a remote place where they were less likely to be harassed by those who were hostile to them. Their journey to their new home is described under the entry on Brigham Young. *See* YOUNG, BRIGHAM.

MOUNTAIN MEN

Mountain men was a term applied to the fur trappers of the west, particularly those who were independent as opposed to those who were employees of one of the fur-trading companies. It was quite common for the so-called mountain men to marry Indian women.

N

NAUVOO

Nauvoo in Illinois was the place to which the Mormons went when they moved from Missouri in 1938. Situated on the banks of the Mississippi and a virtual swamp when the Mormons arrived there, Nauvoo in a remarkably short time became one of the most flourishing communities in the country. There the Mormons under the leadership of Joseph Smith tried to create an ideal society with the aim of creating an independent state.

NAVAHO *or* NAVAJO

The Navaho Indian people were among the many Indians who were badly treated by white people who wanted for themselves the land inhabited by the Indians. The Navahos were not wholly innocent, of course, and were wont to steal horses and sheep in the area that they inhabited. This was in the southwest where the states of New Mexico, Arizona, Colorado and Utah meet.

In 1863, during the Civil War, Kit Carson was ordered by General Carleton to subdue the Navaho. This did not appear to be an easy task as the Navaho were difficult to capture in their native mountains and canyons. Carson tried to get them to move to the reservation at Bosque Redondo, an arid area of land near the military outpost of Fort Sumner in New Mexico, telling them that if they did not go of their own accord they would be pursued and destroyed.

They did not surrender and Carson kept his word. He ordered their crops and peach orchards to be destroyed, their homes to be burnt and their sheep to be rounded up. Winter came and the Navaho began to freeze and starve. In the spring of 1864 most of the Navahos surrendered. About 6,000 of them had to march 300 miles to the Bosque Redondo, this march becoming known to the Navahos as the Long Walk.

Conditions were far from comfortable at the reservation. The land was poor and could not support the number of Indians who were forced to live there. Many of the Navahos died from disease or lack of food. Still they were forced to stay there for four years.

After four years, in 1868, they were allowed to return to their homeland if they gave their word that they would not break the law of America or defy the authorities. When they returned to their homeland they were given sheep and tools so that they once again could make their own living. They became one of the most populous Indian tribes in America.

NEZ PERCES
The Nez Perces (Pierced Noses) were an Indian people who for a long time enjoyed amicable relations with the white men. They lived in the Wallowa Valley and trouble arose when the government tried to take this away from them. The story of this is told in the entry under Chief Joseph. *See* JOSEPH, CHIEF.

O

OAKLEY, ANNIE
Annie Oakley was a performer in William Cody's Wild West Show, which began in 1883. She was born Phoebe Ann Moses to a Quaker family in Darke County, Ohio. She became extremely expert with a gun and appeared as the second act after Cody, known as Buffalo Bill. She was known as Little Sure Shot and was noted for her ability to shoot cigarettes out of men's mouths. Such a markswoman was she that she could split playing cards from thirty paces. She was married to Frank Butler, a marksman whom she once beat in a shooting competition. They performed together for some time, Annie Oakley being in Cody's show for seventeen years. The film *Annie Get Your Gun* was based on Annie Oakley. *See* CODY, WILLIAM.

OK CORRAL
OK Corral, which was located in Tombstone, Arizona, is remembered in the history of the West for the gunfight that took place near there. The gunfight featured the famous Wyatt Earp and his brothers, Morgan and Virgil, and Doc Holliday. They killed three gunmen of the gang known as the Cowboys. The story of the fight is told under OK Corral at the entry at Wyatt Earp. *See* EARP, WYATT.

OREGON TRAIL

The Oregon Trail was brought into prominence by John Fremont who, with Kit Carson, travelled overland to Oregon through Nevada across the Sierra and into California. He then made a map of the area and a lengthy and glowing report of it.

Migration to Oregon had begun on a small scale in the late 1830s; more pioneers followed in the early 1840s. After Fremont's expedition and the publicity it attracted, a great many more people set off for Oregon, particularly in view of the fact that the Panic of 1837 had bankrupted so many people in the east and mid-west that they were anxious to make a new start. Between 1845 and 1847, between 3,000 and 5,000 optimistic people started out along the Oregon Trail. Many of them were farmers from Missouri and Iowa who had hit hard times.

They set out on wagons pulled by oxen and mules, taking as many of their worldly possessions as they could, sometimes including cows and chickens, and provisions for the journey. The caravans of wagons left from towns along the Missouri River, such as Independence, St Joseph or Westport, now Kansas City. The aim of many of the travellers was to set out as soon as the grass was high enough to feed the livestock.

To reach the Cascade Mountains by October and so avoid the worst of the snows, the caravans had to aim to travel fifteen hours a day. The route first cut northwest across the prairies of eastern Kansas. Because of the likely weather conditions it was important to try to keep to some kind of schedule, and about 45 days after leaving the Missouri River behind the travellers on the Oregon Trail aimed to reach Fort Laramie where they could refit their wagons and obtain supplies. From Fort Laramie the trail led northwest along the Platte River and headed west.

OURAY

Ouray was one of the chiefs of the Utes. *See* UTES.

OUTLAWS

The wide open spaces of the West were almost tailor-made for
those trying to escape the law. Frequently crimes were committed far from towns and official guardians of the law, and, even if
the perpetrators of crime were captured, it was easy for them to
disappear. In addition, the opening up of the West gave many
opportunities for outlaws to commit crimes, such as cattle-rustling, bank raids and the holding-up of trains and stagecoaches.

Another factor in the rule of the outlaw in the West was that it
was difficult for communities to get competent lawmen, given
the level of violence in many of them. Often the only people
prepared to take on the lawkeeping role were those who had
themselves known what it was like to be outside the law.

An interesting point about the West and outlaws was the level
of sympathy that there was for many of them. This was partly
because the outlaws often robbed what were seen as the institu-
tions of the establishment and these were often an anathema to
ordinary people. For example, there were people, such as farmers, ranchers and businessmen, who resented banks not only in
principle but also because in many cases they had been refused
loans by them—they resented the power that the banks had over
peoples' lives. When it came to trains and stagecoaches there
were people who resented their role in opening up the land to an
ever-increasing number of immigrants. Cattle-rustling was another crime for which many people had sympathy because there
was much resentment against the rich cattle barons who had
taken over the ranges that were really public land.

So it was that outlaws such as the James gang were admired
rather than reviled. Stories went round about them being along
the lines of Robin Hood but, although they may have robbed the
rich there is little evidence that they gave their loot to the poor.

In addition to the romanticism that was associated with outlaws, there came a significant degree of exaggeration. Indeed,

the exaggerated exploits of outlaws, the number of hold-ups they took part in, the number of people they shot, and so on, were an important, integral part of the myth of the West.

P

PANIC OF 1873
A financial panic broke out in Kansas in the late summer of 1873. It had looked like being a good season for the cattlemen but the cattle market collapsed quite suddenly and several cattle drivers and shippers were made bankrupt. The market recovered but the temporary collapse of the cattle trade had marked the end of Ellsworth as the principal cow town in Kansas. Other financial panics occurred in 1837 and 1857.

PARKER, CYNTHIA ANN
Cynthia Parker in 1836 was borne off as a captive by Comanche raiders from Parker's Foot in Texas when she was nine years old. When she was eighteen she became the wife of Chief Peta Nocona and bore him two sons, Quanah and Pecos, and a daughter, Topasannah.

In December 1860 when the Nocona were camped near the Pease River and while the men were away hunting, a force of Texas Rangers and US cavalry struck. They carried off Cynthia Ann and her daughter and took them back to her uncle and brother. Far from being overjoyed, she missed her sons and tried to escape on several occasions in order to join them. In 1864 when her daughter Topasannah died Cynthia Parker starved herself to death.

PARKER, QUANAH
Qhanah Parker was the son of Cynthia Ann Parker. His father,

who was Chief Peta of the Nocona, died of an infected arrow wound and his mother was taken back to her own people where she starved herself to death from grief at being separated from her sons. To add to his tragedy, his brother, Pecos, died of a disease, probably cholera.

Quanah joined the Quahadi, a warlike band of the Comanche who were extremely hostile to white people. When the majority of soldiers were removed from Texan forts and sent to fight in the Civil War and with them many other Texan men, the Quahadi Comanches set out to devastate the area by burning houses, farms and ranches to the ground and killing hundreds of settlers.

During these Comanche attacks of the 1860s Quanah became a war chief of the Quahadi, second only to Bull Bear. He was totally opposed to the idea of living on a reservation and refused to take part in the peace talks of 1867. Instead he and his men continued to maraud Texas, returning to their hideout at Staked Plains in the Texas Panhandle.

The authorities were determined to stop him and assigned Colonel Ranald Mackenzie to conquer him and any other rebels in September 1871. However, Mackenzie was not used to fighting the Indians and he had not legislated for Quanah's habit of making sudden raids on the army and then vanishing instead of engaging in a confrontational fight which would have suited Mackenzie better.

Quanah was a fearsome fighter when ready for battle. He was large and very powerfully built and he painted his face with black war paint.

Mackenzie, however, kept up his campaign against Quanah despite setbacks and, after a necessary respite for the winter, he began trying again to subdue the Comanche in March 1872. In September he attacked the camp of the Kotsoteka Comanche and killed many warriors and even more women and children.

The morale of the Kotsoteka was very low and many of them went to live on the reservation. Even Quanah and the Quahadis felt disinclined to fight.

For a while there was peace but white buffalo hunters who had practically stripped Kansas of buffalo began to turn their attention to Texas and set up a base near the deserted trading post of Adobe Walls. The Indians felt that they had to defend their land and their buffalo from such hunters. In addition, the governor of Texas had asked for five Comanche braves to be surrendered to him for a raid that had taken place. The Comanches refused. It did not look as though peace would last much longer.

In Spring 1874 a council of Indians took place at Elk Creek, organized by Quanah. A Quahadi medicine man, Isa-tai, made a prophecy that one all-out attack would drive away the white hunters and protect the buffalo and the Indian lands. Quanah is said to have been sceptical of the prophecy but the Indians agreed on a mass attack on the buffalo hunters at Adobe Walls.

The weapons that the Indians had, however, were no match for the modern long-range rifles that the buffalo hunters had. The courage of Quanah and his men was not enough to win the battle and they failed to gain access to the stockade. After an unsuccessful siege, the Indians withdrew, having lost many men.

Those Indians who survived continued to carry out raids on the southern plains but the army harassed them without giving them any time to rest. They burned the Indian camps, destroyed their supplies and slaughtered their ponies. After a particularly severe rout by the white men in September 1871, the Indians had had enough and they began to go to the reservations.

The last to do so were the Quahadis. Quanah and his men held out until he received a message from Mackenzie that if he surrendered the Quahadis would be treated honourably but if he persisted in fighting the Quahadis would be exterminated. In June 1875 Quanah arrived at the reservation at Fort Sill with his men, having agreed to surrender. *See* ADOBE WALLS and PARKER, CYNTHIA ANN.

PARKER, ISAAC

Isaac Parker was known as the 'hanging judge' because of the severity of his sentencing. In his time as a judge he is said to have sent 168 men to the gallows with 89 of these being reprieved. He had a particular inclination towards mass or multiple hangings and was known to have hanged four or five men at a time.

He was appointed by President Grant in 1875 to clean up the Western District, which was centred on Fort Smith and had jurisdiction over the Indian Territory, now Oklahoma. This was an area with a great many outlaws as well as around 50,000 official Indian inhabitants.

Despite his reputation for harshness and sternness, he was a friend to the Indians and tried to treat them fairly. He is also generally held to be have been relatively free from corruption, although corruption was rife in the lawmen of the West and skill at their job very low.

Judge Parker had a difficult task. The Indian Territory was a favourite area for criminals and outlaws to hide out between jobs. It was a situation that called for stern measures. He appointed 200 deputies and tried to select as honest men as possible although this was no easy task. He worked six days a week himself and in a period of twenty-one years he tried 28,000 suspects.

There were many complaints about the severity of his sentencing. In time the extent of his jurisdiction was lessened in size and his powers were decreased further when prisoners were allowed to appeal to the Supreme Court after sentencing.

He died in 1896, having been in ill-health for some time. One of the Creek Indian chiefs is said to have brought wild flowers to his funeral to put on his grave.

PARKER, ROBERT LEROY *see* CASSIDY, BUTCH.

PONY EXPRESS

When people started migrating to the West in great numbers, such as happened during the various gold rushes, communication became a distinct problem. The distances involved were very great, there was not yet a transcontinental telegraph system and it would be some considerable time yet before the Atlantic and Pacific coasts were linked by rail.

One solution to the problem was the Pony Express. This was the idea of William Russell, a partner in a freighting firm, and it began operating in April 1860. Its aim was to have a relay of horsemen who would take the mail between Missouri and California, a distance of about 2,000 miles, in ten days.

There were 25 'home stations', at which the riders were changed, about every 75 miles, and about 165 'swing stations', at which riders changed horses, about every 15 miles. The Pony Express riders were young, their age averaging about nineteen, and one of them was to become famous as Buffalo Bill (William Cody). They had to be fit as well as being young, as it was such a punishing journey over very difficult terrain, including the Rocky Mountains, the Utah Desert and the Sierras.

It is remembered as a glorious enterprise typical of the spirit of the frontier but it was a short-lived venture. It was not that the Pony Express was unsuccessful—in fact its record time for delivery was 7 days 17 hours—but that it was overtaken by the technology of the time. In October 1861 the Pacific Telegraph Company and the Overland Telegraph Company completed the transcontinental line and made the Pony Express redundant.

From then on a message east to west or west to east could take seconds.

The Pony Express is part of the legend of the West but Russell and his partners lost thousands of dollars on the enterprise and received nothing from the government. Their reward for the ingenious scheme was bankruptcy.

PINKERTON NATIONAL DETECTIVE AGENCY

The Pinkerton National Detective Agency was founded as a private police force by Allan Pinkerton, a Scots immigrant. The agency was on the side of the Union in the Civil War and helped with its secret-service operations and just before the Civil War had gained fame by foiling a plot to assassinate Abraham Lincoln.

The agency grew quickly in the late 1860s and the early 1870s. It became involved in the disputes between management and workers in the coalfields of Pennsylvania when it helped to destroy a workers' terrorist organization known as the Molly Maguires.

Pinkerton detectives also became involved in tracking down the robbers of the West. The Reno brothers, who were the first people in the world to hold up a train, were apprehended by Pinkerton detectives, John in 1867 and William and Simeon in Canada in 1868. In order to get their men, the Pinkerton detectives sometimes tried to infiltrate gangs of robbers. A Pinkerton operative tried to infiltrate the James-Younger gang and was killed. Then another operative was killed in a gunfight with the Younger brothers.

The Pinkerton detectives, whose motto was 'We never sleep', were often regarded with great hostility. In particular, the attack by some of their operatives on the house of the mother of the James brothers in which she was injured and their half-brother was killed, brought them into ill-repute. Jesse James had a great hatred for Allan Pinkerton and vowed to kill him, although he died before him.

The agency had some spectacular successes. For example, they succeeded in getting Butch Cassidy and the Sundance Kid to Bolivia. Their success may have been in part a result of the fact that they sometimes used ex-gunfighters, such as Tom Horn, but they were not unique in this since many official law officers in the West were ex-gunfighters.

Pinkerton died in 1884 and he left the business to his sons, William and Robert. By that time there were offices in several cities throughout America. Although the operators were still active against outlaws in the 1890s, many others were being employed by employers to help them take action against militant workers.

In several cases the Pinkerton operatives infiltrated the militant organizations or unions with a view to reporting the supposed troublemakers to the employers and they became very unpopular. Charles Siringo was one of these and he was later to write autobiographical accounts of his life, both as a cowboy and as a detective. Eventually, in 1937, Pinkerton's had to abolish their industrial division after Congress ruled that industrial spying was illegal. *See* SIRINGO, CHARLES.

Q

QUAHADI
The Quahadi were a branch of the Comanches. Quanah Parker joined them on the death of his father and brother and became one of their war chiefs. He led them into battle against the white men. *See* PARKER, QUANAH.

QUANAH *see* PARKER, QUANAH.

QUICK, FLO

Flo Quick was one of several women in the West who are known to have adopted male clothing. She called herself Tom King and was an outlaw, being a cattle rustler in the Indian Territory. As well as being an outlaw in her own right, she was the mistress of an outlaw, Bob Dalton. When she was Dalton's mistress she acted as a spy for his gang. Using the alias Eugenia Moore or Mrs Mundy, she struck up a friendship with employees of the railroad companies in order to find out information on the trains, information that was then passed on to the Daltons. After Bob Dalton's death, Flo Quick set up a gang of her own. She is said to have been shot either in a gunfight or in a hold-up, dressed as a man.

QUANTRILL, WILLIAM CLARKE

During the American Civil War there was a great deal of guerrilla warfare conducted as well as more formal, official warfare. Much of this took place in Missouri, and one of the most noted of the guerrillas was William Clarke Quantrill. The Union forces occupied St Louis and many other strategic places in the state of Missouri, many people from Missouri having Confederate sympathies and being on the side of the south. One of these was Quantrill.

He was noted for his acts of atrocity, which were so horrible that they appalled even people who were Confederate supporters. In one act of atrocity Quantrill's band of men attacked Lawrence, Kansas, in August 1863 and murdered 150 civilian men and boys.

Quantrill's men included 'Bloody Bill' Anderson, who was the leader's right-hand man. Frank James who, with his brother Jesse, became a notorious outlaw was also a member of Quantrill's gang at one point, as were the Younger brothers.

R

RAILROADS

The railroads played a major part in the opening up of the west. As people became excited by the idea of a new life in the west and began to migrate there in earnest in the 1840s, serious attention began to be given to the provision of a transcontinental railway. The dream of a transcontinental railway was further fuelled by the discovery of gold in California. People thought how wonderful it would be if truckloads of gold could be hauled east by rail from the goldfields.

Central Pacific Railroad

In 1861 the dream was on its way to realization. The Central Pacific Railroad was founded in that year by four businessmen from Sacramento, California. They were Charles Crocker, Mark Hopkins, Collis P. Huntingdon and Leland Stanford, Governor of California.

Union Pacific Railroad

A year later they were granted a charter by Congress for the building of a railway from Sacramento going east. At the same time, funds were also assigned for the building of the Union Pacific Railroad in the east, starting from Nebraska and going west.

Workers and problems

The laying of rail track required a great many workers, especially as the work was being carried out at such a rate. Charles Crocker of the Central Pacific Railroad was instrumental, through his Chinese manservant, in employing a great many Chinese workers on the building of the Central Pacific Railroad.

Meanwhile the railway from east to west was being built by a crew consisting of Irish immigrants and Civil War veterans.

It was extremely hard work through extremely difficult terrain and their equipment was rudimentary. Furthermore, there was potential danger from Indians and the inclemency of the weather conditions to contend with. The two teams worked particularly quickly because they were in competition with each other, the first to complete its part collecting a government grant.

Joining of the railroads

Eventually the two teams met at an agreed spot, Promontory, Utah. The date was 10 May 1869. The final spike was made of gold and it was laid by Leland Stanford. A dream had come true—it was now relatively easy to travel from east to west and back again. The West would never again seem so impenetrable.

RANGE DETECTIVES *see* RUSTLING.

RANGE WARS

Range wars was the term applied to the struggle between the major ranchers, or so-called cattle barons, and the homesteaders. This centred to a large extent on the problem of rustling and the best-known range wars were in Johnson County and Lincoln County. *See* JOHNSON COUNTY WAR and LINCOLN COUNTY WAR.

RED CLOUD

Red Cloud (1822–1909) was a Sioux warrior chief who opposed the expansion westward by the white men. In 1865 the American government decided to open a road to the Montana goldfields along the Bozeman Trail. When soldiers were sent to prepare a way for the new road they were continually harassed by Red Cloud and his men and the soldiers withdrew. The reason for the harassment was that the Bozeman Trail ran through the middle of Powder River country, the last part of Sioux land where the buffalo roamed free.

Bozeman Trail

Early in 1866, Colonel Henry B. Carrington of the Eighth Cavalry was appointed to the task of overseeing the building of a system of forts along the Bozeman Trail in Wyoming. Conscious of the opposition that he would encounter from the Sioux, Carrington asked the Sioux leaders with other Indian leaders to join some members of the federal government in a meeting at Fort Laramie. It was the aim of the white men to get the Sioux to part with the rights to the Bozeman Trail.

The deal was supposedly that, if the Indians guaranteed a safe passage to the passage of white travellers on the Bozeman Trail, the Indians would receive $75,000 a year and a promise that their land would never be taken by force. However, Carrington appeared with a column of men and wagons and explained that he was going to build more forts on the trail. At this Red Cloud stormed off, saying that he would fight for the last hunting grounds of his people.

Sniping

Red Cloud was as good as his word and harried the white men mercilessly as they built their forts. By the time they were building Fort Phil Kearny, the whites were being killed or wounded at the rate of one a day. The Sioux continued to make sniping attacks but Carrington tightened up his security significantly.

Fetterman Massacre

In November 1866 a young infantry captain named William Judd Fetterman joined Carrington and was foolhardy enough to think that he could take on Red Cloud and his men. The result was a rout of the white men at Lodge Trail Ridge, a rout that was in fact a massacre which became known as the Fetterman Massacre.

Wagon Box Fight

In the late summer of 1867 there was another battle between the white men and the Sioux at Fort Phil Kearny. The battle was known as the Wagon Box Fight because Captain James Powell had built a barricade of large wooden boxes taken from the wagon beds so that some of his men could shelter behind them when Red Cloud and his braves attacked them. The odds were overwhelmingly against Powell and his men from the point of view of numbers but they won the battle because of the new weapons that they had—breech-loading Springfield rifles. These enabled them to withstand the Indian attack until reinforcements arrived. Red Cloud lost many of his best fighting braves.

Treaty of Fort Laramie

Red Cloud must have thought that it was all over for him after this defeat, but the authorities still feared him and were anxious to placate him. They wanted to sign a treaty with Red Cloud but he refused to sign it until the authorities agreed to withdraw soldiers from the forts in Sioux country. They acceded to his demands and he signed the treaty at Fort Laramie in 1868.

By the terms of the treaty, Red Cloud and his people were to settle on a large reservation in Dakota and to refrain from hostilities against the white men. In return, the American government agreed to abandon the Bozeman Trail, the cause of the hostilities, Red Cloud seeing it as a threat to the hunting grounds of his people. They also agreed to designate as 'unceded Indian country' the Powder River country and to allow the Sioux to have the Black Hills of Dakota for 'as long as the grass shall grow'.

Red Cloud retires

They were not to keep their word. The white settlers were furious at the government's concessions to the Indians and felt that the Indians had been given the best land and more trouble was to come. Red Cloud, having travelled to Washington with twenty other Sioux chiefs to discuss the situation, realized the scale of the white men's power and reluctantly gave up warfare and went to live in a reservation south of the Black Hills in Dakota.

In time he adopted the dress and speech of the white men, as did many others. However, he still had a concern for his own people and tried to lobby the government with a view to improving the conditions of the American Indians.

Red Cloud may have decided to give up his old ways and stop harassing the white men. However, other Sioux made other decisions, among them Sitting Bull. Under his leadership, and that of Crazy Horse, the Sioux continued their struggle against the white men. *See* Crazy Horse; Sioux and Sitting Bull.

REGULATORS

The Regulators was the name adopted by the society formed by the Wyoming Stock Growers' when they decided to take vengeance on people whom they considered to be rustlers. The forming of this society under the leadership of Major Frank Wolcott led to the Johnson County War. *See* Johnson County War and Wyoming Stock Growers' Association.

RENO BROTHERS

The Reno brothers were train and bank robbers whose gang was smashed by the Pinkerton Detective Agency. The brothers were responsible for the first train robbery in America when they boarded a train in Indiana in 1866 and held it up.

RODEOS

The word 'rodeo' is Spanish in origin, the Spanish word meaning a gathering place of cattle. Rodeos originated from people displaying the traditional cowboy skills, especially with a view to proving that their skills were superior to those of someone else or other people. For example, it was quite common for men who had driven cattle up the trails from Texas to Kansas to take part in informal competitions in cow towns such as Abilene, Dodge City, Ellsworth, etc.

Many of the rodeo events involved the competitor in pitting his strength, stamina and wits against livestock, for example, lassoing or roping cattle, riding unbroken horses or bucking bronchos, etc. William Cody, known as Buffalo Bill, added to the popularity of rodeos and made them more organized. In his *Old Glory Blowout* on 4 July 1882 held in North Platte, Nebraska, he succeeded in getting local merchants to donate prizes for a number of rodeo-style events, and then on 4 July 1883, a rodeo event was held in Pecos, Texas, at which cash prizes were given for the first time.

Rodeos grew in popularity in the West and are still popular in America today. Gradually they added more in the way of razzamatazz to what was originally a display of the skills needed to survive on the ranch.

Women also played a part in rodeos, particularly from the beginning of the century on, and in the early days they competed against men on an equal basis. Among the early famous female rodeo competitors were Prairie Rose Henderson, Prairie Lillie Allen and Lucille Mulhall.

ROGERS, ROY

Roy Rogers (1912–), who was born Leonard Slye in Cincinnati, Ohio, was a western film actor who became known as the King of the Cowboys. He was one of the best known of the western film actors known as 'singing cowboys'. In fact, he began his career in the entertainment industry as a singer and performed with several bands in the 1930s before moving on to combine singing with cowboy skills, which he improved upon by spending some time on a ranch in Montana

He starred in more than a hundred films, legally changing his name to Roy Rogers in 1938. Before that he had appeared in films under three different names: Leonard Slye, the name given to him at birth, Dick Wooten and Roy Rogers. His first starring role was in *Under Western Skies* (1938). Rogers owes some of his rise to fame and popularity to the fact that Gene Autry, also a singing cowboy screen actor, went off to serve in World War II, leaving the stage clear for Roy Rogers, so to speak.

With his second wife, Dale Evans, he was part of a screen partnership that was widely regarded as being a role model for the perfect family life, violence being kept to a minimum in their films. The first film in which the couple appeared together was *The Cowboy and the Senorita* (1944), three years before they were married.

The Rogers/Evans partnership increased in popularity with the advent of television. They appeared regularly, always displaying the virtues of the wholesome family couple. Rogers himself subscribed to the same moral code as that of Gene Autry in his 'Ten Commandments of the Cowboy'. *See* AUTRY, GENE and EVANS, DALE.

ROSE OF THE CIMARRON

In the Indian Territory in the 1880s and 1890s there flourished a number of female outlaws. One of these was known as Rose of the Cimarron. She was the mistress of the outlaw George Newcomb, who was nicknamed Bitter Creek, whom she had met when she was fifteen. Newcomb was a member of Bill Doolin's gang and Rose is supposed to have assisted him to escape from a gunfight in Ingalls, Oklahoma, in 1893 by hiding a gun and cartridge belt under her skirt and running over to give them to him.

Newcomb was killed in a gunfight in 1895. The men who were responsible for his death were none other than Rose's brothers, who killed him for the reward that had been put up for his capture or death. *See* DOOLIN, BILL.

RUSSELL, WILLIAM

William Russell was the person who conceived the idea of the Pony Express, by which mail was delivered east to west and vice versa by a relay of young men on horseback. The Pony Express began operating in April 1860 but because of the completion of the transcontinental telegraph line lasted only about 18 months. Russell, who had thought of it as a good moneymaking scheme to pay off some of his debts, was left worse off than he had been before. The person to whom his firm owed most money, stagecoach operator Ben Holladay, foreclosed and Russell became bankrupt, as did the company of which he was a partner, Russell, Majors and Waddell.

Earlier, in 1855, Russell, with partners Majors and Waddell, had started a freight wagon service from St Joseph to San Francisco that developed very rapidly and successfully. Unfortunately the company lost money, supposedly because the army reneged on payment and Russell was too much of a financial gambler.

Before the Pony Express venture, Russell had hit upon the idea of capitalizing on the goldrush by establishing a stagecoach line to Denver. He therefore set up the Leavenworth and Pike's Peak Express Company. His usual business partners, Majors and Waddell, had no faith in the viability of the project and refused to be involved. Russell found another partner in John J. Jones but, although it was efficient, the project proved not to be viable. Russell was facing bankruptcy and, in order to save their freight company from being brought down with him, Majors and Waddell took over the stagecoach business, reorganizing it as the Central Overland, California. This was in vain, as it happened, as they went bankrupt after the demise of the Pony Express anyhow. *See* PONY EXPRESS.

RUSTLING

Cattle rustling is inextricably linked with the history and the legend of the West. The term was used to indicate the taking of cattle that did not belong to the taker. Rustling, to a greater or lesser extent, occurred on all the cattle ranges of the West. Given the large extent of the ranges, and the difficulty of guarding or policing them, it was not surprising that people were able to steal cattle fairly easily.

Mavericks

The problem intensified as conditions on the range changed. Originally it was accepted that maverick calves could be acquired by anyone and branded as part of his herd, 'maverick' being the name given to an unbranded, seemingly motherless calf. However, people took advantage of this situation and started laying claim to and branding calves that were neither motherless nor ownerless but which simply had not yet been branded by the real owner.

Rebranding

Worse, the practice of rebranding developed. Cattle that had already been branded were taken and had the external branding marked or ironed over by unscrupulous thieves. This could be proved only by killing the animal and examining the inside of the hide, which could still bear the trace of the original branding.

Not all rustlers appropriated cattle to rear as stock or to sell it to others who would do so. Many of them simply stole the cattle, buried the telltale branded hides and sold the beef.

Homesteaders and the cattle war

The Homestead Act of 1862 encouraged settlers to go west. Under the act any citizen over the age of twenty-one could claim up to 160 acres of what was public land. If he lived on it for five years and showed his intention to put the land to good purpose, for example by building a house, fencing off the land and so on, then he became the owner of the land.

The take-up on this offer was slow to start with but in the 1870s and the 1880s there was practically a stampede to become homesteaders. The ranchers objected to the fencing off of land and held that the homesteaders were liable to rustle cattle. On the other hand, many of the homesteaders resented the power and wealth of the ranchers as well as the extensive nature of their grazing lands, and many were not above doing a bit of rustling on this basis.

Vigilantism

One of the results of rustling was that the major cattlemen often took the law into their own hands when it came to punishing the people whom they believed to be rustling. The lawmen in the west tended to lack training, to be ineffective and to be corrupt, and, more importantly from the point of view of the cattle ranchers, they were often far from the scene of the rustling, given the scale of the distances in the West.

The ranchers often employed range detectives who posed as cowboys to look out for cases of rustling. However, even if the ranchers could prove rustling, it was not always easy to get a conviction. Thus ranchers often meted out summary punishments.

This punishment often involved hanging people from trees, as happened with Ella Watson and Jim Averill in Sweetwater County in Wyoming.

The lengths to which the ranchers would go to get revenge on those whom they considered to be rustlers are demonstrated by the events that led to the Johnson County War. The Wyoming Stock Growers' Association formed a society known as the 'Regulators' who drew up a list of people who were considered to have been engaged in rustling and who were to be killed. In order to do this they appointed Major Wolcott to lead a military-style invasion into Johnson County.

Earlier, in Montana, Granville Stuart had set up a group known as the Vigilance Committee, unofficially known as Stuart's Stranglers, and they were ruthless in identifying, tracking down and hanging cattle rustlers and horse thieves.

Cattle rustling may sound bad enough since any theft is a crime. However, the implications of rustling were far greater than simple theft in the West. Rustling caused tempers to run high and violence was often the result.

See AVERILL, JIM; JOHNSON COUNTY WAR; MAVERICKS; MAVERICK ACT; VIGILANTISM and WATSON, ELLA.

S

SACAJAWEA

Sacajawea was a member of the Shoshoni Indians who was captured by the Hidatsa Indians as a child and taken far from her home. She is remembered in the history of the West for having acted as guide and interpreter to Lewis and Clark for part of the way on their expedition (1804–06) from east to west of America after the purchase of Louisiana from the French. She joined the expedition with her husband at Fort Mandan and was of great assistance to the expedition since the expedition's route lay through Shoshoni territory and the members of the expedition needed to acquire horses from them on which to cross the Rocky Mountains. *See* Lewis and Clark Expedition.

SAMUEL, ZERELDA
Zerelda Samuel was the mother of Jesse and Frank James. She was badly wounded, and her son by her second marriage to Reuben Samuel, Archie Samuel, was killed during an attack on her house in 1875 by members of the Pinkerton Detective Agency when they were trying to track down the James brothers. *See* James, Jesse.

SAND CREEK MASSACRE
Sand Creek in 1864 was the scene of a massacre inflicted on members of some of the Indian tribes, including the Cheyenne and the Arapaho, under the direction of Colonel John Chivington. The Indians had gone there in peace, many of them had already surrendered their weapons and the totally unexpected attack took place at night. Chivington was later condemned for the massacre by a military board but he went unpunished, since he had left the army by that time. *See* Arapaho.

SHANE
Shane is the title of a classic western novel (1949) by Jack Schaefer. The film (1953) based on the novel has also become a western classic. It was directed by George Stevens and starred Alan Ladd. The plot centres on the theme of homesteaders versus the cattle barons and their hired gunmen.

SCHAEFER, JACK WARNER
Jack Warner Schaefer (1907–91) is remembered in the cult of

the West as the author of the classic western novel *Shane* (1949). He wrote several other western novels and collections of stories, such as *The Canyon* (1953) and *Monte Walsh* (1963), and some of them, like *Shane*, were made into films. However, none of them achieved the long-term fame that *Shane* did.

SINGLETON, BENJAMIN ('Pap')

Benjamin Singleton (1809–92), better known as 'Pap', was an African American who was instrumental in persuading many African Americans to leave their homes in the south and settle in the West, particularly in Kansas. His idea was that they should take advantage of the Homestead Act of 1862 by which the government would grant up to 160 acres of land to anyone over twenty-one who was prepared to live on the land for at least five years.

Singleton was born into slavery in Nashville, Tennessee, in 1809 and is said to have been sold more than twelve times as a young man. He ran away three times but was captured each time until he finally succeeded in escaping to Canada. He did this by means of what was known as the Underground Railroad, a system by which a series of sympathetic householders provided shelter for runaway slaves who were making their way to freedom.

After the Civil War he returned to Tennessee hoping to see great improvements. However, he was horrified to see the poverty that his people were still enduring, although they were now free. It was this that made him dream of helping them to make a new and better life elsewhere to the extent that he had thousand of leaflets printed giving details of the homestead scheme. The people who followed his advice and went to Kansas were known as Exodusters.

The Exodusters met with varying fortunes. Singleton was to regret that not more people had joined him in the West and that

not more had made a success of the venture. He was later to
think that perhaps the African Americans in the southern states
of the United States would be better to set up colonies in Africa
but that idea did not meet with a great deal of enthusiasm. Singleton died a poor man in Topeka, Kansas, in 1892 at the age of
eighty-three. *See* EXODUSTERS.

SIOUX

The Sioux were an Indian people of which there were several
tribes, such as the Huncpapa, of which Sitting Bull became a
warrior chief, the Oglala, the Santee and the Teton. They played
an important part in trying to prevent the white man from ex-
ploiting the West, particularly their own lands.

The Oregon Trail ran through the southern territory of the
Sioux, and troops were garrisoned at Fort Laramie in case the
Sioux seemed disposed to attack the migrating settlers in their
wagons. At first they showed little sign of doing so. The start of
real trouble centred on what was originally a trivial incident.

A group of Mormons were travelling along the trail on their
way west in August 1854 when a worn-out, lame cow wandered
off the trail and became lost. A young Sioux warrior, named
High Forehead, presumably assuming it to be a stray, shot it and
butchered it. On hearing of this, the owner of the cow demanded
payment but this was not granted by the chief, although he is
said to have offered two cows, or two horses, as reparation. The
matter was reported to Lieutenant Hugh Fleming at Fort
Laramie but he did not pay very much attention.

Death and the start of conflict

Unfortunately Fleming was persuaded by a young lieutenant,
John Grattan, to allow him to go to the Sioux village with a
troop of men to settle the matter. He was young and arrogant
with a contempt for the Indians. He demanded that the chief

hand over High Forehead but High Forehead was a guest in the village and the chief refused. Grattan ordered his men to fire point-blank into the Indian village. Swarms of Indians surrounded the troops when they fired. The troops were all killed but one, and he died two days later of his wounds. The war between the Sioux and the white men had started and it was to last over thirty-five years.

Santee Sioux
The Santee or eastern Sioux were located in Minnesota. The amount of land that they had been left with by the government was very small, simply a strip of rather barren land about 150 miles long and 10 miles wide on the south of the Minnesota River. The government had taken about 26 million acres from the Santee Sioux in exchange for an annual cash payment. Unfortunately the cash payment was woefully inadequate and it was difficult for the Sioux to live on it.

Deprivation
Worse, however, was to come. The annuity, small as it was, failed to arrive in the summer of 1862. This blow was on top of the fact that the Santees' corn crop the previous year had been virtually destroyed by cutworms and that the local traders were unsympathetic and would not extend credit to the Indians. The Indians were starving and the white traders would not help. There was much worry and frustration among the Santees and tempers ran high.

War
Things came to a head in August when a group of young braves dared each other to shoot a white man. Coming across a group of white settlers, the braves shot them—three men and two women. They then went and reported the matter to their leader, Little Crow, who called a council to debate the issue.

Little Crow and some of the other chiefs were against war, partly because of the sheer number of white men vis-à-vis the Santees. However, others argued for war, partly on the grounds that there would never be a better time, since so many white men were away engaged in a war against each other, the Civil War. Those in favour of war won and Little Crow agreed.

At dawn the next day, 18 August 1862, the Santees went on the rampage and killed many people, many of them unarmed; women were raped and houses burnt. The white people who survived made for Fort Ridgely on the north side of the river. The commander there took out a force of men to deal with the Sioux but the troops ran into an ambush and were all killed. In all 400 white settlers died because of the actions of the Santee Sioux up until then.

Little Crow then attacked Fort Ridgely, which by then had been reinforced. He and his braves were repulsed and many of them were killed. The Santees then attacked the town of New Ulm and reduced the town to ashes. Whites in the area were in a state of panic.

Defeat

Troops under the leadership of Colonel Henry Sibley, a former fur trader, were sent against the Santees. As the troops progressed, the Indians kept up their skirmishes, but Little Crow and his men were defeated by the army on 22 September near Wood Lake. Little Crow and many of his men left for the Plains, although some went to the reservation. The chief was killed by a farmer some time later, although it is said that the farmer did not know the identity of the chief at first.

Retribution

Sibley rounded up 2,000 Santees, some of whom had not taken part in the uprising. Of these 400 were tried, many of the trials being very short, and more than 300 were condemned to die by hanging. A local Episcopal bishop appealed to President Lincoln to intervene and Lincoln commuted the sentences of all but 38 of them, those who had been convicted of murder or rape, as opposed to those who had taken part in battle.

The Santee reservation by the Minnesota River was then abandoned and the 2,000 Santee Sioux were sent to a small reservation by the Missouri where there were already 3,000 Winnebago Indians.

Later conflict
This was by no means the end of the saga of the Sioux and the white men. There was to be more war. For details of other conflicts *see* CRAZY HORSE; GHOST DANCE; RED CLOUD; SITTING BULL and WOUNDED KNEE.

SIRINGO, CHARLES ANGELO
Charles Siringo I (1855–1928) is remembered as the author of the first cowboy autobiography, *A Texas Cowboy or Fifteen Years on the Hurricane Deck of a Spanish Pony* (1885). It was an authentic account and was popular with the public. He went on to publish other books based on his adventurous life as a cowboy and detective, many of them using autobiographical detail.

Siringo was born in a small settlement in Texas. He became a cowboy at the age of eleven and stayed one until the age of twenty-six. After that he had another adventurous career as a member of the Pinkerton Detective Agency and in pursuing this career he had to infiltrate a miners' union in Idaho in order to report back on the more militant of the miners who were out to cause trouble for the owners of the mine. This proved a dangerous job as the miners discovered the identity of the person who had been informing on them and he had to flee for his life. His evidence was to convict eighteen union leaders. *See* PINKERTON DETECTIVE AGENCY.

SITTING BULL

Sitting Bull was a member of the Huncpapa Sioux. He was originally a medicine man, called Sitting Bull, or Tatanka Iyotake, because he was slow and deliberate. Sitting Bull's power increased among the Sioux after Red Cloud's retirement.

Discovery of gold

Red Cloud had signed an agreement with the government that the Black Hills of Dakota would belong to the Sioux for 'as long as the grass shall grow'. The government was already going back on its word when gold was discovered in the Black Hills in July 1874. Prospectors rushed there, demanding that the Sioux be removed. Meanwhile the Sioux demanded that the prospectors be removed from their hallowed land. The government tried to take the heat out of the situation by offering to buy the Black Hills from the Sioux for $6,000,000 or, alternatively, by leasing the mining rights at $400,000 a year. Red Cloud and the other reservation Sioux refused both offers.

Reversion of treaty

The white prospectors went ahead with their mining schemes anyhow and began to set up mining towns in the Black Hills. They even demanded the removal of the Sioux. President Grant decided to placate the whites rather than to keep his word to the Indians. He therefore signed an order demanding that all Indians leave the unceded land and go to live on reservations by 31 January 1876 or they would be treated as being hostile and forcibly driven in. By this means did the government lay claim to both the Powder River country as well as the Black Hills.

Gathering of forces

Blizzards and bad weather generally held up the delivery of this message to the Indians and many of them did not meet the deadline, whether or not they would have been inclined to do so. An army began to assemble with the intention of subduing Sitting Bull and his men. Meanwhile Indians were gathering from all over the northern plains to meet in the Powder River country. Sitting Bull's camp had by this time expanded greatly. Not only were many of the Sioux tribes represented there but also the Arapaho and some of the other Indians from the northern plains.

Sitting Bull's sun dance and vision

In June 1876 Sitting Bull decided to hold a sun dance. His adopted brother, Jumping Bull, cut pieces of flesh from his arms with a sharp knife, after which Sitting Bull danced for eighteen hours with his eyes firmly fixed on the sun until he fell down in a trance. He claimed to have seen a vision of many soldiers falling into his camp upside down and construed this vision as meaning that the soldiers were dead and that God would send the Indians victory.

The Battle of Rosebud and the Battle of Little Bighorn

Not long after Sitting Bull's sun dance was over, some scouts reported that they had seen General Crook with a troop of soldiers in the valley of the Rosebud River. Crazy Horse was in charge of the Sioux and Cheyenne warriors, Sitting Bull being still weak from the sun dance, and defeated Major Reno on 17 June 1876. The Indians celebrated the victory and then went on to defeat General Custer at Little Bighorn a few days later. For details of the latter encounters see the entry at Crazy Horse.

Canada and surrender for Sitting Bull

The Indians won the battles but they paid a high price. They were harassed by all the experienced Indian fighters in the army and gradually they surrendered. Crazy Horse surrendered in May 1877 but Sitting Bull and Chief Gall and a band of the Huncpapa Sioux had decided not to go to a reservation but escaped to Canada hoping to find refuge. Their Canadian venture, however, did not work out and they faced hunger, disease and disagreements. Sitting Bull and a band of his followers finally had had enough and they surrendered and went to the reservation at Fort Buford in Dakota, ragged and hungry, in July 1881.

Ghost dance and death
This was not the last that was to be heard of Sitting Bull. He was to play a part again in the struggle of whites against Indians. He expressed an interest in having his braves taught the ghost dance, which Wovoka of the Paiutes had brought to the Indians, after having been told about it by the Great Spirit in a vision. His involving himself in the ghost dance alarmed the white authorities. The resultant manhandling and arrest of Sitting Bull led to his death, details of which are given in the entry at ghost dance in the section on Sitting Bull. His death in turn led to the tragedy of Wounded Knee. *See* CRAZY HORSE; GHOST DANCE; SIOUX and WOUNDED KNEE.

SMITH, JOSEPH
Joseph Smith (1805–44) was the founder of the Church of Jesus Christ of the Latter-Day Saints, better known as the Mormons. *See* MORMONS.

SODBUSTERS
Sodbusters was the derogatory name given to the settlers on the Great Plains who went there with the intention of farming the land. Some of these did so under the auspices of the Homestead Act, by which the government would grant up to 160 acres of land to anyone over twenty-one who was prepared to have a go at farming the land for at least five years and some were squatters with no legal claim to the land. Either way, they were regarded as a nuisance by the ranchers, particularly when they

began to fence off the land that the ranchers had always made use of for their stock

STARR, BELLE

Belle Starr (1848–89) was born Myra Belle Shirley in Missouri. She became one of the West's most notorious female outlaws, being known as the Bandit Queen. As well as being an outlaw herself and staging robberies and stealing cattle, she was also the lover of several outlaws. Cole Younger of the James-Younger gang was one of these and Belle claimed that he was the father of her daughter, Pearl.

She was also the lover of Jim Reed, who took part in some of the James-Younger gang's raids, and had another child, Edward, by him. He was killed either while resisting arrest or for the reward that had been offered for him.

Belle then had her own gang for a while before opening a livery stable in Dallas. She then took up with a Native American Indian, Blue Duck, before going to live with another outlaw, Sam Starr, who was part Cherokee. Whether or not she actually married him, she adopted his name. They lived on the Canadian River and welcomed people on the run to their cabin.

In 1883 Belle was sentenced by Judge Parker to nine months' imprisonment for being the leader of a band of horse thieves. After her release she went on stealing horses and robbing. Sam Starr was killed in 1886 in a gunfight with a lawman and Belle took up with a Creek Indian outlaw known as Jim July.

Then in 1889 Belle was shot in the back. Who the assassin was has not been absolutely established, although several sources lay the blame at the door of one of Belle's neighbours, Edgar Watson, with whom she had had a difference of opinion over a piece of land. Another possible suspect was her son Edward with whom she was supposedly having an incestuous affair.

STRANGLERS, STUART'S *see* STUART, GRANVILLE.

STUART, GRANVILLE

Granville Stuart from Virginia was originally a gold prospector who had made the first gold strike in Montana in 1858. In 1879 he started a ranch in Montana on the Yellowstone River with a range on what had been the best of Indian hunting grounds.

The ranges in Montana were as prone as those in Wyoming to rustling and rebranding. In order to protect their property, the Montana ranchers organized themselves into the Montana Stock Growers' Association and Stuart became leader of it.

Their attempts to employ range detectives and to get the cattle thieves convicted in the courts failed and Stuart tried another method. He formed the Vigilance Committee of fourteen stockmen, which met secretly at his house. They were assiduous and ruthless in identifying, tracking down and punishing cattle rustlers. Punishment was by hanging and a placard was always left indicating that the person hanged was a cattle thief or a horse thief.

The Vigilance Committee became known as Stuart's Stranglers and was much feared. By 1884 rustling in the Montana-Dakota range had practically been abolished—estimates of hangings were as high as seventy-five—and the Vigilance Committee was disbanded. Vigilantism, however, was to be practised elsewhere on the ranges and was the cause of the Johnson County War in Wyoming. *See* VIGILANTISM.

SUNDANCE KID

The Sundance Kid was the name given to Harry Longbaugh or Longabaugh, friend of Butch Cassidy and fellow member of the gang known as the Wild Bunch. He was from Pennsylvania but migrated to Wyoming when he was in his teens. He served a prison sentence in the Sundance Penitentiary for horse-stealing and worked as a cowboy on a Wyoming ranch before joining the gang. The rest of his story is told at the entry on Butch Cassidy. *See* CASSIDY, BUTCH.

SUTTER, JOHN

John Sutter (1803–80) was born Johann Augustus Sutter in Switzerland. He arrived on the Pacific coast of America in 1839 and obtained a large land grant in the Sacramento Valley in California. He then built a fort that was named Sutter's Fort. In January 1848, when a carpenter named James Marshall was building a sawmill for Sutter, he found some shiny particles in the millrace and took them to Sutter. These proved to be gold.

Sutter was aware of the damage that could be done to his land and buildings if armies of people came in search of gold and he tried to keep news of the gold find quiet. This proved impossible and the news spread, largely thanks to Sam Brannan, a local merchant, who saw marvellous opportunities for his business to make money selling tools and supplies to prospectors. People flocked to California when President James Polk in December 1848 confirmed that gold had been found there.

The California goldrush had begun and the term forty-niner coined. *See* GOLD RUSH.

SUTTON-TAYLOR FEUD

The Sutton-Taylor feud was a bitter family feud between the Sutton family and the Taylor family and took place in De Witt County in Texas. Such feuds were common in the West and, as was the case with the Sutton-Taylor feud, the origins were often obscure.

The main reason that the feud between the Suttons and the Taylors is remembered as part of the history of the West is because of the involvement of John Wesley Hardin, a notorious outlaw and noted hard man and gunfighter. Hardin decided to take the part of the Taylors and in his autobiography devotes quite a lot of space to the feud

In 1873 he shot Captain Jack Helm, supposedly one of the most prominent of the supporters of the Sutton family, claiming that Helm and his gang, including Bill Sutton, had murdered a number of men. It has also been claimed that Helm had tried to shoot Jim Taylor and that Hardin was retaliating. So terrified of Hardin was everyone that none of Helm's friends who were standing by attempted to retaliate.

Hardin regarded Bill Sutton as his deadly enemy but he had always eluded him. On hearing that Sutton was going to Kansas to sell some cattle, he advised Jim and Billy Taylor to try to get Sutton at Indianola. Jim Taylor shot him in the head as Sutton boarded a steamer. Friends had horses waiting, and he and Billy Taylor, who had shot Sutton's friend, Gabe Slaughter, escaped.

The Sutton-Taylor feud survived long after Hardin had ceased to be involved in it. Thirty years later, when most of the original participants had long gone, it came to an end.

T

TA RANCH

The TA Ranch played an important part in the Johnson County War. It was to where Frank Wolcott and the Regulators retreated when they were made aware that Sheriff Angus and a posse of Johnson County townspeople were out to get them, having heard of the Regulators' treatment of Nate Champion and Nick Ray. The Regulators barricaded themselves into the TA Ranch and had almost given up hope of withstanding the siege when Colonel J. J. Van Horn and three troops of the Sixth Cavalry arrived. *See* JOHNSON COUNTY WAR.

TELEGRAPH SERVICE

In October 1861 the Pacific Telegraph Company and the Overland Telegraph Company of Hiram Sibley completed the transcontinental line. This was to help greatly in the opening up of the west since it was to make east-west communication so much easier and accessible. The completion of the telegraph line was to bring to an end an enterprising venture known as the Pony Express, a mail system using a relay of young riders. *See* PONY EXPRESS.

TEXAS RANGERS

The precursors of the rangers were raised in the 1820s in what was still Mexican territory to protect the new American settlers from the Comanches who resented the arrival of settlers on their land. Then Stephen Austin, leader of the Anglo-American Texans, raised a body of armed mounted men in 1826 as a defensive force. These were referred to as 'watchmen' or 'rangers' but not yet as Texas Rangers.

The term Texas Rangers was applied in 1835 and the numbers of the defensive force was increased to around twenty-five. Their remit was to 'range and guard the frontier between the Brazos and Trinity Rivers', and a short time afterwards their area of jurisdiction was extended westwards to the Guadalupe River.

During the Texas Revolution (1835–36) their numbers were increased even more, to around 150, and they played an important part in defending Texas when it became a republic. They defended the Texan settlers not only against the Indians, being involved in several victories over the Comanche, but against any Mexican raiders.

The rangers had to provide their own horses, their own saddles and blankets. In addition their pay was very meagre—$1.25 a day. Being a Texas Ranger was clearly not a profession that would make men wealthy but it was an exciting, adventurous life, and several of them, including Captain John ('Jack') Coffee Hays, became legendary figures of the West. They did not wear an uniform and were the first civilian force to use Colt's revolvers.

The Texas Rangers were disbanded after the Mexican War and the American army took over the role of protecting the settlers against the Comanche. The Rangers continued to operate unofficially and were reorganized officially again to fight the Indians. Their task also included capturing Mexican bandits and capturing and returning runaway slaves.

After the Civil War the Texas Rangers, who had been on the side of the Confederates, were once again officially disbanded. At first the disbanded Union Army was in charge of providing frontier protection and then this role was taken over by the Texas State Police, a body that was largely composed of ex-slaves and so very unpopular locally. There was a great deal of lawlessness and disorder in the state and there was a great deal of demand for the Texas Rangers to be brought back.

In 1874 the Texas Rangers were revived. A frontier battalion was raised under the leadership of Major John B Jones to fight the Indians and a 'Special force of Rangers' under Captain Leander H. McNelly was raised to quell the lawlessness and disorder along the Texan border with Mexico. The Rangers were noted for their courage and effectiveness. They were famous for getting their man and they captured many outlaws and criminals.

The Texas Rangers were much admired but they had their faults. In particular they have been accused of discrimination against Hispanic people on both sides of the Texan-Mexican border and of representing only the interests of the powerful Texan ranchers.

The role of the Texas Ranger was to track down outlaws but it was not unknown for a ranger to be an outlaw. One such was James Miller, gunfighter and murderer, who was a resident Texas Ranger at Memphis, Texas, in the late 1890s. He was the killer in February 1908 of Pat Garrett, himself an ex-Texas Ranger, who killed Billy the Kid.

The Texas Rangers are still in existence, although on a much smaller and less active scale than in their heyday.

THOMAS, HECK

Heck Thomas (1850–1912) was born in Georgia and served on the Confederate side in the Civil War, having joined the Stonewall Jackson Brigade of the Confederate Army at the age of twelve. After the Civil War he went to Texas and worked as a private detective and then went to Oklahoma to serve as a deputy under Judge Parker.

He was one of the Oklahoma Guardsmen appointed by Marshal Evett Nix, along with Bill Tilghman and Chris Madsen, to help clean up Oklahoma by tracking down the outlaws. Thomas is particularly remembered as the lawman who shot the outlaw Bill Doolin. Details of this are given in the entry on Bill Doolin. *See* DOOLIN, BILL.

THOMPSON, BEN

Ben Thompson (1843–84) was a gunfighter who was born in Yorkshire. In the Civil War he fought on the Confederate side with the Second Texas Cavalry and then served with Emperor Maximilian in Mexico. He was extremely skilled in the art of using a gun and was an inveterate gambler.

Abilene

In 1871 he and Phil Coe opened a gambling saloon called the Bull's Head Tavern and Gambling Saloon in Abilene. They had a difference of opinion with Wild Bill Hickok over the rather lewd picture of a bull used to advertise the saloon but this was settled amicably by Hickok altering the picture slightly with paint to make it less offensive.

Ellsworth and Bill

Ben Thompson then moved to Ellsworth and joined forces with his brother, Bill. Bill had a great capacity for getting into trouble and such was Ben's devotion to him that he spent some considerable time getting him out of trouble.

Sterling and Morco

A classic example of Bill's capacity for trouble is a tragic one. In August 1873 Ben had staked a fellow gambler, John Sterling, in a gambling game on condition that he would get half of the winnings and the return of the stake if Sterling won. Sterling did win $1,000 but he evaded Ben Thompson and went to Nick Lenz's saloon. Thompson, hearing of his win, tracked Sterling down and demanded his money but Sterling slapped his face.

One of the local lawmen, 'Happy Jack' Morco, who disliked Texans in general and the Thompson brothers in particular, leapt between Sterling and Thompson to save Sterling from retribution. He pulled his gun and forced Thompson, who was unarmed, to leave the saloon.

Thompson made for Brennan's saloon and Sterling and Morco, both heavily armed, arrived. Thompson then ran to Jack New's saloon for his own guns. At this point Bill Thompson appeared with Ben's shotgun, having had a great deal to drink. Bill discharged a hail of buckshot and nearly hit two innocent bystanders. Ben tried to lead Bill to the railroad where they could fight without endangering others.

Death of Whitney

Sheriff Chauncey Whitney, who was a friend of the Thompson brothers, rushed to stop a fight and persuaded the brothers to go back to Brennan's saloon. When they were there someone shouted to Ben Thompson that Morco was coming and that he was armed. Ben ran out in the street and fired but Morco ducked into a store.

That was when tragedy struck. Bill dashed out into the street with Whitney behind him. Still suffering from the effects of having drunk too much, he turned round and shot Whitney. Ben was distraught at the shooting of his friend but realized that his brother was in danger and pushed Bill on to a horse to get out of town before the crowd could take vengeance on him.

Ben then faced the crowd and agreed to surrender his weapons to Ed Hogue, another of the lawmen in the town, if Morco also was disarmed. Whitney died an agonizing death three days later, saying until the end that the shooting was an accident. It was not until 1877 that Bill was brought to trial. He was acquitted, some say because the jury members were bribed, some say on a technicality.

Austin, Texas

As for Ben, it was claimed in later years that Wyatt Earp actually arrested him but the records do not appear to bear this out. The claim seems simply to be part of the myth and legend that grew up around many of the well-known figures in the West, such as Wyatt Earp.

Ben later became marshal of Austin, Texas, and succeeded in reducing the crime rate there, partly because of his reputation as a gunfighter. He was popular with the townspeople but he had to retire from his post after he had a gunfight with an old enemy of his in San Antonio. He met a violent death, being murdered in 1884. Ben Thompson is regarded as one of the great shots of the West and was acknowledged as such by Buffalo Bill (William Cody), who was defeated by Thompson in a pistol-shooting match.

Details of Bill's death are not on record. It has been suggested that he was killed in a gunfight near Laredo, Texas, in the late 1880s.

THOMPSON, BILL *see* THOMPSON, BEN.

TILGHMAN, WILLIAM

William, better known as Bill, Tilghman was a lawman. He was one of the few lawmen in the west who made a professional career of the job, who became very effective and who survived long enough to demonstrate this.

He was marshal in Dodge City from 1884 until 1886, and in 1889 became the first marshal of Perry in Oklahoma. Under the direction of US Marshal Evett Nix, he joined Heck Thomas and Chris Madsen, who was Danish by birth and who had fought with Garibaldi, been in the French Foreign legion and been in the American Cavalry before becoming a lawman in Oklahoma, as part of the Oklahoma Guardsmen, or the Three Guardsmen as they were known.

Their task was put an end to the exploits of outlaws such as the Doolin gang, particularly those of Bill Doolin. The story of Tilghman's capture of Doolin is told under the entry on Bill Doolin. Later Tilghman shot another member of the Doolin gang, Dick West, in a gunfight in Kingfisher County, Oklahoma, in 1897.

Tilghman had a long and distinguished career in Oklahoma and was responsible for much of the cleaning-up process there. He was much respected and was voted a state senator. At the age of seventy he was shot by a gunman and died a few minutes later from the wound, the scene of his death being Cromwell, a wild oil town in Oklahoma, where he had become marshal. He had heard a shot in the street and went out to remove the gun from the gunman but, unknown to Tilghman, the gunman had another gun with which he shot him. *See* DOOLIN, BILL.

TOMBSTONE

The town of Tombstone, Arizona, is best remembered in the history and legend of the West for its association with Wyatt Earp. The town is said to owe its name to a prospector called Ed Schieffelin, who was once told that the only thing that he would find when he was prospecting in the Dragoon Hills was graves. When he found substantial veins of silver in the area in 1877 he decided to name his claim Tombstone in memory of the warning given to him.

Its name was not the only thing that silver prospecting gave to Tombstone. It also brought a great deal of trouble and lawlessness as the miners sought to make a great deal of money. In December 1879 Earp went there at the invitation of his brother, Virgil, who was deputy marshal there. His other brothers, Jim, Morgan and Warren, also moved to Tombstone.

Tombstone is particularly remembered as the town where the OK Corral was situated. It was near there that the gunfight to which it has given its name was fought on 26 October 1881 when the Earps and their friend, Doc Holliday, took part in the gunfight against some of the gang known as the Cowboys, including Ike and Billy Clanton. The Earps' opponents were all killed in hardly any time at all. *See* OK CORRAL.

TUBBS, 'POKER ALICE'

'Poker Alice' Tubbs (1851–1930) was a famous woman gambler in the West. She was an Englishwoman, born in Suffolk in 1851, the daughter of a schoolmaster, who went to America when she was twelve. She married a mining engineer, Frank Duffield, in Colorado when she was nineteen. When he was killed in a mining accident, she took up work as a schoolteacher but augmented her income by dealing cards in a saloon on a percentage basis, becoming noted for the large cigars that she smoked.

William Tubbs

She soon began to work for Bob Ford, the killer of Jesse James, but on Ford's death she moved to Deadwood where she worked as gambler alongside William Tubbs. Men were frequently fooled into thinking that it would be easy to beat a mere woman at cards, especially one with such a refined accent and so wrongly assumed to be inexperienced at gambling.

Alice not only adopted the male habit of smoking cigars but also adopted the male habit of carrying a gun. This was to come in useful when a drunk miner attacked her gambling partner with a knife after accusing him of cheating at cards. Before the miner could do any damage with the knife, Poker Alice shot him in the arm, making him drop the knife.

Tubbs and Alice married and settled down to raise chickens, having adopted seven orphans. Soon afterwards Tubbs died of pneumonia and she tried to make a living in sheep farming before she once again began gambling for a living. She married again but the marriage lasted only a short time.

Club-owner and killer

Next she opened a club near Fort Meade in South Dakota. Her career as a club-owner was successful but it was brought to an end when she killed a man. Some soldiers who were very drunk were trying to gain admittance to her club after hours. She thought that their intention was to rob her and she shot through the door to deter them. Unfortunately one of the men fell dead.

Poker Alice was tried but the judge, although he found her guilty, let her go free in view of her age. She then retired to a farm and died at the age of seventy-nine in the course of a surgical operation.

TUNSTALL, JOHN HENRY

John Henry Tunstall (1853–78) was an Englishman, the son of a wealthy London merchant, who settled in New Mexico in 1876, having been first in Canada and then California before that. He chose Lincoln County to settle in and played a major part in the Lincoln County War. *See* LINCOLN COUNTY WAR.

U

UNFORGIVEN

Unforgiven (1992) is a western film starring and directed by Clint Eastwood.

It tells the story of William Munny who was raising his two children on a Wyoming pig farm after his wife died of smallpox when he was told of a reward that was being offered for the killing of two cowboys who had cut up a prostitute. Munny sets out to try and claim it but comes up against Sheriff Little Bill Daggett. It is a powerful film which, as is the case with other of Eastwood's films, has scenes of great violence. *Unforgiven* won two Oscars, one for best film and one for best director.

UNION PACIFIC RAILROAD

The Union Pacific Railroad line started at Omaha, Nebraska, and went towards the west over the Great Plains. The workers on the railroad were mainly Irish and there was much competition between them and the Chinese layers of the Central Pacific Railroad's line. This resulted in extremely fast track-laying, particularly on the part of the workers on the Central Pacific line. The Union Pacific line and the Central Pacific line finally met at Promontory Summit in Utah on 10 May 1869.

A series of shanty towns grew up along the rail-track, many of them being dismantled as one section of track was finished and reassembled farther on. The makeshift towns provided saloons for drinking and gambling and there was much prostitution.

UPSON, ASHMAN
Ashman Upson was the ghostwriter of Pat Garrett's rather fanciful *The Authentic Life of Billy the Kid* (1882).

UTAH
The territory of Utah was the site, in the Salt Lake area, where the Mormons settled after their march west. It was also the site of the reservation assigned to the Ute Indians in 1879. *See* MORMONS; UTES; YOUNG, BRIGHAM.

UTES
The Utes were an Indian tribe whose territory covered what is now western Colorado and southeastern Utah. Their location was a rugged mountain area. The appearance of the horse in their territory , probably around 1650, changed the Utes' way of life. Stray horses from the ranches or cattle trails formed wild herds of mustangs and were captured by the Utes. They used them to hunt the buffalo on the plains below their homes and to go on marauding raids. Before that the Utes were a poor tribe who scraped a living by hunting and gathering.

When the Utes were scattered across Colorado and causing trouble to the authorities in the Rocky Mountains region, the chief of one of the Ute tribes, Ouray, who was more inclined to talk than to make war, settled on the Los Pinos reservation and was given a salary to act as a government interpreter .

In order to try to bring all the Utes under control, the government officials hit upon the plan of appointing Ouray as chief of all the Utes and of officially assigning boundaries of land to the Utes. By this treaty (1863) they lost most of their deer-hunting ground. Kit Carson was sent to Colorado in order to make use of his peacemaking skills and became a friend of Ouray and the two went on a trip to Washington together.

However, the government in 1872 persuaded Ouray to sign away a good deal of the territory which the Utes had acquired under the treaty of 1863 in exchange for a farm, house and generous annual salary for himself. The Utes were furious and were still furious at the start of what was called the Utes' War in 1879.

The Utes were incensed at the high-handed way in which the agent in charge of the White River reservation, Nathan Meeker, was treating the Utes who lived there. Trouble flared and the Utes attacked a troop of cavalry under the leadership of Thomas Thornburgh, killing Thornburgh and a number of others. They then attacked the reservation, massacred Meeker, and carried off his wife and daughter. Ouray was powerless to stop them.

In 1879 a new governor of Colorado was appointed who was very much against the Utes. They were banished to some desolate land in Utah which the Mormons considered to be too barren to house people. The reservation there was called after Ouray, although he did not live there, preferring his comfortable house and farm in Colorado.

V

VAQUERO
A vaquero was the Mexican equivalent of a cowboy.

VIGILANTISM
Vigilantism was common throughout the West. This was hardly surprising in view of the level of lawlessness that existed and the lack of official law-enforcers in some areas. Some areas

were very remote and extensive so that it was difficult to enforce the law. Other areas, such as the cow towns of Kansas, were so violent that people were understandably reluctant to become law-enforcers there.

This combination of lawlessness and lack of lawmen often spelt vigilantism. Summary justice was often meted out, for example, in the case of rustlers and horse thieves. The distance involved in getting criminals involved in these activities were considerable and the crimes were sometimes difficult to prove. In the state of Montana in one year alone, 1884 local ranchers had at least 35 suspected rustlers executed without any form of trial.

Hanging the offenders on the spot without benefit of trial or jury seemed an acceptable expedient option, although of course, as is the case with vigilantes, the dispensers of on-the-spot-justice did not always bother to find out that the punishment was being meted out deservedly. Sometimes the supposed justice meted out was extremely cruel and there were cases of rustlers being tied to trees and burned to death.

Mob rule often reigned and lynchings were by no means uncommon. If a crowd thought that someone was guilty of rustling, horse-thieving, murder or some other crime, they simply took a piece of rope and hanged the suspect on the nearest tree. Such lynchings were sometimes referred to as 'necktie' parties. One famous example of lynching by vigilantes was that of Jim Averill and Ella Watson, believed to have been organized on behalf of the Wyoming Stock Growers' Association by Albert Bothwell, although he was never indicted.

Vigilantes did not operate only on a casual ad-hoc basis. They were frequently quite organized, almost an official police force. One of the most terrifying vigilante movements in the west was the group of cowboy vigilantes known as Stuart's Stranglers. Their focus of interest was the Montana-Dakota range territory and when they disbanded in 1884 they had virtually wiped out cattle-rustling from the area.

Even more formally organized was a kind of secret society formed by the Wyoming Stock Growers' Association under the leadership of former American Army Major Frank Wolcott in 1892. They called themselves the Regulators and were virtually a private army and aimed to execute a large number of homesteaders in Johnson County. Their action led to the Johnson County War. *See* AVERILL, JIM; HOMESTEADERS; JOHNSON COUNTY WAR; WYOMING STOCK GROWERS' ASSOCIATION and VIOLENCE.

VIRGINIAN, THE

The Virginian is a well-known early western novel by Owen Wister (published in 1902) and a film (1929) starring Gary Cooper. It then became the basis of a TV series in America in 1960. *The Virginian* made a folk hero of the cowboy, although the picture of cowboy life that it presents is highly romanticized, and many other writers then copied this image of the cowboy. *See* WISTER, OWEN.

VIOLENCE

Violence plays an important part of the myth of the West in book and film. It also played a significant part in the reality of the West. Whether the West actually was as violent in reality as it came to be in myth is open to dispute, and certainly the myth of book and film has glamorized the violence, but in any event the West had many of the ingredients that violence breeds on.

Drinking and gambling were both common in the West in the cow towns, in the mining towns and in the temporary shanty towns constructed as the railroad workers laid track. Either separately or in combination, both contributed to the violence, as did ready access to weapons. Men quarrelled and reached for their guns or knives. Death was frequently the result. Not surprisingly it was often difficult to get lawmen to take up posts in these towns, and frequently the authorities appointed people who themselves had been outside the law.

Gangs of outlaws contributed to the violence of the west and even more to the violent myth of the west. Frank and Jesse James and the Younger brothers and others, such as the Dalton brothers, achieved notoriety as they held up trains and stage-coaches and robbed banks, killing anyone who tried to stop them. Certainly their way of life was violent but to many people who did not want the railroads to open up the country and who were deeply suspicious of banks, they became folk heroes. Even in their lifetimes the extent of their violence was probably exaggerated.

Violence often resulted from people taking the law into their own hands. There was a lack of law officers and many crimes, such as cattle-rustling and horse-thieving, took place in remote areas that were far from the towns where lawmen were located. In such cases violent summary justice was often meted out by vigilantes. Hanging the suspects from trees or tying them to trees and setting fire to them were favourite ways of bringing retribution.

Whilst it is true that many people died as a result of violence in the west, many more died of the harsh conditions that existed there. In particular many people died of injuries sustained in the course of their work, there being a distinct shortage of doctors and medical facilities, particularly in the remote parts.

Cowboys ran the risk of being thrown from horses, of being kicked by horses, of being gored by bulls, or of being crushed by stampeding cattle. Those people involved in gold-mining were also subject to dangers at work, these including mine cave-ins and falls down shafts. Trappers were subject to the vagaries of the weather and attacks from Indians. *See* OUTLAWS and VIGILANTISM.

W

WAYNE, JOHN

John Wayne (1907-79), known as 'the Duke' was a film actor specializing in western films who came to epitomize the cinema cowboy. He appeared in around 250 films, his first major film being *Stagecoach* (1939). *Stagecoach* was directed by John Ford, as were many other films in which John Wayne starred.

Born Marion Michael Morrison in Winterset, Iowa, Wayne was at the University of Southern California when he began taking summer jobs at the Fox film studios and was soon offered parts as a screen extra. He appeared in several westerns from the studios of Republic Pictures before appearing in *Stagecoach*.

Wayne depicted the cowboy as a hero, as someone who epitomized the American ideals. He was a fervent patriot and an ultraconservative. He helped to found the anti-Communist Motion Picture Alliance for the Preservation of American Ideals in 1944 and in 1948 became its president.

The Duke had a loyal following, although his ultra-conservatism brought him criticism. It was a considerable time before he won an Academy Award but he did so with *True Grit* (1969).

Regarded as the last of the great traditional cowboy filmstars, he died of cancer in 1979, three years after having played a gunfighter dying of cancer in *The Shootist* (1976).

WATSON, ELLA

Ella Watson, who changed her name to Kate Maxwell, was a Canadian-born prostitute from Kansas who ran a saloon in Sweetwater County in Wyoming and was widely regarded as accepting unbranded, or maverick, cattle in exchange for her services as a prostitute to stock a small ranch which she ran near her saloon. She attracted the wrath of the powerful Wyoming Stock Growers' Association, which is said to have organized a vigilante group under Albert Bothwell to lynch her and her partner, Jim Averill, by hanging them from the branch of a pine tree on Spring Creek Gulch in July 1889. *See* AVERILL, JIM and WYOMING STOCK GROWERS' ASSOCIATION.

WELLS FARGO
Wells Fargo was a freight company started by Henry Wells and William Fargo. It was the major transporter of gold and silver in the west and the largest stagecoach firm. Their stagecoaches were subject to attacks and hold-ups by outlaws, and the company frequently offered rewards for the capture of the outlaws and even employed their own detectives to track down the culprits. In common with other freight companies, it employed agents as representatives in all the major western towns.

WELLS, HENRY *see* WELLS FARGO.

WICHITA
Wichita was one of the Kansas cow towns, which became famous and infamous for a relatively short time in the 1870s during the heyday of the cattle trails. Most of these towns were points where trail-drivers from Texas deposited their herds so that the beef could be carried back east for processing and sale.

As the railroads extended westward, the importance of one cow town faded in favour of another. Thus Ellsworth enjoyed a few years as a boom town and then lost out to Wichita, which in turn gave way to Dodge City.

The end of the cattle trails spelt the end of the boom for towns such as Wichita, but for many of the trades people of the town it was good while it lasted. With Texan trailmen, stock-buyers and land speculators around there was a great deal of money in the town, and saloon-keepers and prostitutes did particularly well. However there was also a good deal of lawlessness and violence, the combination of gambling and heavy drinking often leading to fighting.

WILD BILL HICKOK *see* HICKOK, JAMES BUTLER.

WISTER, OWEN
Owen Wister (1860-1938) was the writer of the early classic western novel *The Virginian* (1902). It had a strong influence on novels about the wild west and did much to create the romantic view of the cowboy's life, which was to play such a major part in literature about the American West.

Wister studied music but his father insisted on him becoming a clerk and he became ill. To recover from a nervous breakdown, he travelled and spent much time in Wyoming. He was so impressed by the landscape and life there that he returned several times, and it became the inspiration for his writing.

As well as *The Virginian*, he wrote several short stories depicting life in the west, and these tend to present a more realistic, less stylized picture. In later life he grew disenchanted with the west and looked elsewhere for inspiration. *See* VIRGINIAN.

WOLCOTT, MAJOR FRANK
Major Frank Wolcott was originally from Kentucky and a former army major. In early spring 1842 he was elected as leader of the Regulators, a secret society, actually a vigilante organization, formed by the Wyoming Stock Growers' Association. Wolcott himself was the owner of a large ranch in the area. It was Wolcott's task to put together an army of gunmen to go to Johnson County and execute about 70 homesteaders and rustlers. This led to the Johnson County War. *See* ANGUS, SHERIFF 'RED'; JOHNSON COUNTY WAR; WYOMING STOCK GROWERS' ASSOCIATION.

WOUNDED KNEE, MASSACRE OF

The Massacre of Wounded Knee happened as a result of the shooting of Sitting Bull and as an indirect result of the mania for ghost dancing which had been introduced by Wovoka, who claimed to have had a revelation in which the Great Spirit had told him to give a dance to the Indians that would bring back the buffalo to the plains and their old proud way of life to the Indians, many of whom were by this time living on reservations and resenting their confined lives.

Ghost dance

The Sioux embraced the idea of the ghost dance with even more enthusiasm than the rest of the Indians in the autumn of 1890 and began wearing 'ghost shirts' with bright-coloured symbols painted on them. The authorities grew nervous, as the chants that accompanied the dancing began to sound warlike. They were particularly nervous when Sitting Bull came out of retirement in October to supervise his braves' ghost dance.

Death of Sitting Bull

The head of the Standing Rock reservation, James McLaughlin, urged that Sitting Bull be arrested to avert further trouble. Accompanied by a troop of Sioux Indian policeman under the leadership of Lieutenant Henry Bull Head, he set out for Sitting Bull's cabin and tried to arrest him to take him to the Fort Yates reservation. One of the Sioux braves shot at Bull Head and he fired as he fell wounded, killing Sitting Bull. There was uproar between the Sioux followers of Sitting Bull and the Sioux policemen, which was stopped only by the arrival of the cavalry.

After the death of Sitting Bull, some of his followers went to the reservation and surrendered but others fled and joined another Sioux chief, Big Foot. The army were keeping an eye on Big Foot because of his enthusiasm for the ghost dance, and they were alarmed when he was joined by Sitting Bull's men.

Meanwhile Big Foot saw the army nearby and thought that it was their intention to attack and kill him.

Big Foot then, in late December, led his people south towards the Pine Ridge reservation with the intention of meeting up with Red Cloud. His party was making for the Badlands of Dakota where he hoped to find two other chiefs, Kicking Bear and Short Bull, with about 3,000 followers who regularly took part in frenzied performances of the ghost dance.

The authorities were now very worried and acted quickly to prevent Big Foot's party from meeting up with the rest of the Indian. They sent Major Whiteside and a troop of the Seventh Cavalry to intercept Big Foot's party. When the army caught up with them on 28 December, Big Foot was ill with pneumonia and suggested parleying but Whiteside insisted on his surrender.

Big Foot agreed to surrender and to lead his people to Wounded Knee Creek. There they were to make camp. During the night reinforcements from the Seventh Cavalry arrived under Colonel James Forsyth.

On the morning of 29 December Forsyth called together the Sioux men and boys. They were wearing their brightly coloured 'ghost shirts', which they believed could protect them from the white men's bullets. The cavalrymen started to search the Sioux tents for weapons but the Sioux squaws were sitting on bundles containing weapons. The troops took as many of the weapons as they could find.

Meanwhile the Sioux medicine man, Yellow Bird, was indicating to the Sioux that he had made a medicine from the white men's ammunition so that the Sioux could not be killed by the white men's weapons if they were wearing their 'ghost shirts'. The medicine man is then said to have thrown a handful of dust and put on his war bonnet.

The soldiers thought that this was a signal for the Indians to attack them. Shots were fired. There were four Hotchkiss guns trained on the Indians' camp and they began showering the Indians with two-pound shells, mowing them down.

It is not known exactly how many people died at Wounded Knee—possibly around 150 Indian men, women and children and around 30 soldiers. Many more were wounded. A blizzard began and the wounded were taken to a field hospital at Pine Ridge. The dead Sioux were left where they lay until the blizzard cleared and they were buried in a common grave.

The rest of the Sioux were gradually persuaded out of the Badlands without more bloodshed, and in January 1891 they laid down their arms to General Nelson Miles at Pine Ridge. There was no more war or resistance against the white men.

WOVOKA

Wovoka is remembered as the bringer of the 'ghost dance' to the Indians. He was the son of Tavibo, a minor chief of the Paiutes in Nevada. His father died when he was fourteen and he was taken to live with a white farmer called David Wilson and was given the name of Jack Wilson.

Wovoka's father had claimed to have revelations by which all the people on earth were swallowed up, only the Indians being resurrected and restored to their old way of life. Before he died he began to speak of the necessity of the Indians dancing in order to get back their old way of life.

The Paiutes were not impressed by Tavibo's revelations but they were more by those of Wovoka, who seemed to inherit his father's gift. During one revelation Wovoka claimed to have been taken up to heaven and told by the Great Spirit to give a dance to the Indian peoples, a dance that would bring back the buffalo and the glory of the Indians' former way of life. The first of dance was performed on the Walker Lake reservation in Nevada in January 1889 and the dance was to spread through the Indian population across the country. *See* GHOST DANCE.

WYOMING STOCK GROWERS' ASSOCIATION

The Wyoming's Stock Growers' Association, formed in Cheyenne in 1873, was a powerful association of wealthy cattlemen. One of the reasons for the forming of such an association was to protect their stock and property and to keep the ranges open.

There was much dispute between them and the homesteaders, both sides claiming to have right on their side. The homesteaders claimed that the large ranchers were trying to keep all the best grassland for themselves and were invading their homesteads with patrols of gunmen. The stockmen claimed that they had invested large sums of money in putting their herds together after the Great Blizzard had destroyed them and that these herds were being rustled by the homesteaders. The problem was that the stockmen had been used to having unlimited use of unfenced ranges for their cattle and they resented the presence of the homesteaders who were fencing the land off, following the Homestead Act.

Detectives

At first the Association employed relatively legal methods to protect their property and stock. They hired men to act as stock detectives. These, sometimes former lawmen but sometimes gunmen, posed as cowboys to spy on the activities of the homesteaders and report back evidence of rustling.

The homesteaders were frequently accused of rebranding the steers that they had stolen. The stock detectives, to prove that this had been done, would skin the hide from the steers that were thought to have been stolen to see if there was evidence of an original brand on the inside, the outside of the brand having been altered by a hot iron by the rustlers.

Even if the stock detectives proved conclusively that rustling had taken place, it was difficult for them to get a conviction. Local people disliked the wealthy stockmen, many of whom were absentee ranchers. The result was that local juries were reluctant to bring a conviction.

Maverick Act

The level of rustling increased, and the association next tried a different tack. They succeeded in having passed the Maverick Act, a 'maverick' being the name given to an unbranded calf, such calves being quite common on the range, particularly if the calf's mother was dead. By this act it became illegal for anyone other than a member of the association to brand an unbranded calf. This act made it illegal for the homesteaders to round up and brand even their own calves without committing a crime.

The Association hired Frank Canton as their chief range inspector. He, although he had been sheriff of Johnson County, had a long history of lawlessness. Inspectors under his leadership incensed the homesteaders by seizing thousands of cattle at markets and shipping points.

Lynching of Averill and Watson

Further, the association decided to take the law into its own hands by lynching people whom they believed to be rustlers to act as a deterrent. They selected as victims Ella Watson and Jim Averill. Ella Watson, who ran a saloon in Sweetwater County, was widely assumed to accept unbranded calves in exchanges for her services as a prostitute, using these to stock a small ranch near her saloon. Jim Averill was her business partner in the saloon and a writer of letters to the local paper, the *Casper Weekly Mail*, denouncing the actions of the ranchers.

Having refused to leave the area under threats, Watson and Averill were seized one night in July 1889, taken to Spring Creek Gulch and hanged from the branch of a pine tree with cowboys' lariats. A local rancher, Albert Bothwell, was widely regarded as being the person who organized the lynching but he was not charged and indeed appropriated Watson's cabin for an ice-house. More deaths followed at the hands of the vigilantes, but the rustling went on.

Major Frank Wolcott

On hearing a rumour that the homesteaders were about to organize an unlawful roundup of cattle, the members of the association decided to take further action to curb rustling. They formed a secret society, known as the Regulators, in spring 1892, and appointed Major Frank Wolcott to head it. This move was to lead to the Johnson County War. *See* AVERILL, JIM, HOMESTEAD ACT; JOHNSON COUNTY WAR, WOLCOTT, MAJOR FRANK.

Y

YOUNG, BRIGHAM

Brigham Young was elected to succeed Joseph Smith as leader of the Mormons, or the members of the Church of Jesus Christ of the Latter-Day Saints, after Smith was murdered in jail in Carthage, Illinois. Young decided that it was too dangerous for the Mormons to go on living in Nauvoo, such was the feeling against them. His plan was to move west to some isolated spot where other people would not bother them. Having studied Fremont's report of the Oregon Trail, he selected the area around Salt Lake City, a distance of about 1,500 miles away.

Omaha

They were to set off at intervals in a series of parties, the first setting out on 4 February 1846, stopping off at a staging camp on the bank of the Missouri River near what is now Omaha. A vast temporary city was constructed so that the 'Saints' could winter there in comfort before moving on. Brigham Young was undoubtedly a skilled organizer but even he could not legislate for the vagaries of the weather.

The winter of 1846–47 was unbelievable in its severity. As many as 700 hundred Mormons are said to have died as a result of exposure, hypothermia, starvation or disease. They were undeterred and an advance party, led by Brigham Young, set out as soon as the first signs of spring appeared. The group was known as the Pioneer Band and consisted of about 150 volunteers.

Deseret
In the foothills of the Rockies they met John Bridger, a trapper, and he told them that parts of the Salt Lake area were too dry for anything other than the cactus. Young decided to aim for the land east of Salt Lake. They arrived there in July 1847 with Young sick with fever. It was agreed that the Mormon state that was to be sited there would be independent and would be known as Deseret, after the Mormon word for bee.

Disaster averted
The soil was very dry but they set about irrigating it by diverting a river. They then planted their crops. In the spring of 1848 they suffered a setback in that, although the crops were doing well, a plague of grasshoppers or crickets appeared. Total disaster was averted when a flock of seagulls appeared and devoured the grasshoppers, thereby saving half the crop.

Converts
Congress refused to accept Deseret as part of the Union but they created the Territory of Utah, included in which was what is now Nevada. Young was declared governor. To boost the population of Deseret, the Mormons dispatched missionaries to make converts to their religion in America and Europe. Prospective immigrants were offered a repayable loan to enable them to get to Deseret. Many thousands went. Throughout the relocation to Utah and throughout the appeal for the immigrants Young showed his organizational and administrative skills.

Gold prospectors and complaints

However, things did not continue to go well. From 1848 thousands of gold prospectors passed through Mormon territory and complained bitterly about the high prices charged there. The prospectors also objected to the high regard in which the Mormons held the native American Indians. So many complaints were made that there arose a high level of antagonism against the Mormons, as a result of which President James Buchanan dismissed Young as governor in 1857 and sent troops to Utah.

Missouri Wildcats

The threat of invasion alarmed the Mormons and reprisals seemed inevitable. At that time, in the late summer of 1857, a group of people were travelling overland with the Fancher wagon. Some of these were bona fide Arkansas farmers but others were some people known as Missouri Wildcats, who routinely reviled the Mormons and some of whom claimed that they had helped in the killing of Joseph Smith.

The Mormons in the southwest of Utah incited the local Indians to attack the travellers as they encamped at mountain meadows near Cedar City on 11 September 1857. A few of the travellers were killed and the rest prepared themselves for a siege. After a few days the Mormons sent word that all was well and the travellers could proceed.

However, this was a trick. As the travellers proceeded through a pass, they were shot down by Indians and Mormons, and within a few minutes more than 100 people lay dead, the only survivors being children. The Mormons panicked and blamed the Indians. No one believed them and a federal army approached. Neither side, however, really wanted the kind of bloody conflict that seemed likely, and Young agreed to step down as governor in favour of a non-Mormon and the army made a token appearance in Utah and then departed.

Thereafter the territory of Utah developed in peace, owing much of its success to Brigham Young.

YOUNGER BROTHERS

The Younger brothers, Bob, Cole and Jim, were outlaws who joined with the James brothers, Jesse and Frank, in all manner of robbery and killing in Missouri and states ranging from Alabama to Iowa. For more than ten years from about 1866, the catalogue of their crimes was phenomenal. They robbed trains, raided banks, held up stagecoaches and broke into banks, sometimes killing anyone who got in their way or tried to stop them.

When the gang decided to try their luck in Minnesota in September 1876, they were not so fortunate. They had decided to raid a bank in Northfield there, but the raid was more problematic than they had bargained for, largely thanks to the courage of the tellers, one of whom escaped to give the alarm. The local inhabitants grabbed what firearms or other weapons they could and descended on the gang.

Some were killed and some injured, Bob Younger being injured quite badly and his horse killed. The Minnesotans went on pursuing the remaining members of the gang. Jesse James wanted to abandon the injured Bob, who was slowing down the escape, but Cole Younger refused and there was a quarrel.

The James brothers then left the other group and managed to escape back to Missouri. The Youngers did not fare so well. They continued to be pursued and were finally cornered by their pursuers. A member of the gang, Charlie Pitts, was killed and the others were so badly wounded that they surrendered.

The Minnesotans took the Younger brothers prisoner and they were sentenced to life imprisonment. Bob died in prison in 1889 and Jim and Cole were released in 1901. Jim took his own life not long afterwards, and later Cole joined Frank James in giving a series of lectures on the evils of crime. *See* JAMES, JESSE.

Index